THE Q BOOK

Practising interrogatives in reading, speaking and writing

John Morgan
Mario Rinvolucri

Longman Group UK Limited,
Longman House, Burnt Mill, Harlow,
Essex CM20 2JE, England
and Associated Companies throughout the world.

© Longman Group UK Limited 1988

First published 1988
Third impression 1989
ISBN 0-582-79606-7

Set in 10/11 pt Century Light

Produced by Longman Singapore Publishers Pte. Ltd.
Printed in Singapore.

CONTENTS

CONTENTS

Oral Work

Writing

ACKNOWLEDGEMENTS

We would like to thank:

Eryl Griffiths and other colleagues at the Cambridge
  Eurocentre
Lou Spaventa
Students at Pilgrims and Eurocentre
Lola and Martin Rinvolucri
Yves Saudrais

Special thanks to Bernard Dufeu to whose work
transmitting psychodrama ideas to foreign language
teaching much of the oral section of this book is due.
His way of working with groups has had a long term
influence on both authors and this goes beyond the
mere teaching of technical ideas.

A hug to all of you!

Also, grateful thanks to the advisers on the project,
whose helpful and constructive comments have been
much appreciated:

Susan Swift
D'Arcy Adrian Vallance
John Flower
David Hill
Eddie Keeling
Teachers in the Language Centre at South Devon
  College of Arts and Technology
Sandra Laucas and colleagues at the Cultura Inglesa,
Belo Horizonte

The Q Book is based on material originally published
by Pilgrim's Publications, Canterbury, 1983.

We are grateful to the following for permission to
reproduce copyright material:

Endsleigh Insurance Services Ltd for an extract from
an 'Accident Report Form'; Guardian Newspapers
Ltd for facsimile of front page, article 'Prison Denial'
by Jasper Becker & article 'Philippine Army and
Guerrillas clash in Weekend of Violence' from *The
Guardian* 23.9.87; Institut Francais de Recherches
Economiques et Sociale/Hachette SA for trans. and
adapted 'IFRES Shopping Survey' from pp 20/21 *Le
Francais Dans Le Monde* October 1984; Macmillan
Accounts and Administration Ltd for abridged
extracts from 'The Earthworm' pp 39–41 *Life;
Form & Function* by C.V. Brewer & C.L. Burrow,
1972; Market and Opinion Research International for
extract from MORI Poll pubd. in *The Times* 28.10.85.
(c) MORI/Times Newspapers; Reuters Ltd for report
from *The Guardian* 23.9.87 and Times Newspapers
Ltd for article 'Warning to the Carpet Cowboy' from
The Times 16.2.83. (c) Times Newspapers Ltd, 1983.

We are unable to trace the copyright holders of the
extract from *Statements on Cinema Attitudes* by
L.L. Thurstone and would be pleased to receive any
information which would enable us to do so.

We are grateful to the following for permission to
reproduce illustrative material in this book:

AA Insurance Service Limited for page 51 (right);
The Diner's Club Limited for page 114; The Guardian
Newspaper Limited for pages 50 and 51 (left);
Irish Tourist Board for page 113; Manpower Services
Commission for page 112; New York Public Library
(The Office of Special Collections) for page 48.

Illustrations on pages 70 and 118 by Andrew Oliver.

Asking questions

Asking a question is a powerful act. When a child asks, 'Mummy, why is the sky blue?' he/she is learning something of that power. Questions can direct the flow of conversation, select the next speaker, compel attention, channel the listener's thought. Authority is vested in those who have the right to ask questions and have them answered: doctors, policemen, teachers.

For the foreign language learner, asking questions is also an expression of power over the language, both in form (interrogatives are far from straightforward in English) and in function (as power over the situation and over other language users). Unfortunately, in many courses, work on questions is highly restricted; at best, practice in 'asking for information' (times, directions, prices etc.), at worst, content-less structure drills. For this reason, in addition to direct practice in interrogative forms (e.g. in the questionnaires and in much of the 'Oral work' section), we have also included activities where question/answer exchanges will arise spontaneously in the learners' production.

This book offers teacher and learner a wide variety of texts and activities where the use of questions is central, but where the emphasis throughout is on meaning and on real (rather than simulated) communication between learners. The exercises are grouped into:

Reading and discussion: learners explore feelings, opinions and knowledge through questionnaires and quizzes.

Oral work: classroom exercises and games to encourage spontaneous oral questions.

Writing: to give learners written practice through answering, expanding and making questionnaires.

How to find your way round the book

It is our intention that this book should be used as a resource in planning classroom work, and not in a linear fashion from start to finish. Each exercise is headed by suggestions regarding learning level, time, and specific language features and an outline description of the topics and language involved (see Table of Contents p 3). In addition, we have tried to take into account the widely differing needs of learners and teachers in different classroom situations. The exercises can be used within either a structural or a communicative language syllabus, and we have paid particular attention to the needs of large classes by including a high proportion of pairwork and small-group activities.

Structure practice

The questionnaires (Sections 1–3, pp 13–79) are naturally 'structure-loaded'; the same structures are used over and over again without any feeling of monotony, unlike the specially constructed passages used to give structural reading practice in coursebooks. Working through them, the learner is led gently to the acquisition and guided production of question forms. There is also ample practice in tense sequencing and 'verb + verb' patterns.

In Section 4 ('Oral work', p 81) and Section 6 ('Writing', p 105), question-and-answer work forms the basis of freer practice.

Reading

Reading in a foreign language can be a daunting business and learners often plough through text without any clear goal in view. The exercises in Sections 1–3 require the learner to be active and involved while reading, e.g. to answer questions about themselves, or to accept or reject parts of the text. Their reading is mixed, sentence by sentence, with a thinking, evaluating and decision-making process. In pairwork, the reading of the questions is broken up and brought to life by the answers one's partner gives. We feel that this book tackles one of the main problems in foreign language reading – the fact that it *is* a daunting experience.

Guided production

Learners are too often presented with external, unasked-for text. They have too little time in class to exteriorise their own internal text; the things *they* have to say, want to say, never before knew they wanted to say. Questionnaires are one way of using external text to trigger and guide text produced by the learners themselves. When A puts a set of questions from the book to B and B gives personal answers

(Section 1, pp 13–43) or when a teacher gives a dictation that has to be completed in a personal way ('Personalised dictations', Section 5, pp 93–103), there is a balance between external and internal text.

Topics and values

Younger learners need to express themselves in a whole range of areas important to them, including their beliefs and values. If yours is an upper secondary class, for example, then read the introduction to the 'Values' section (pp 57–79) and three or four of the units that follow. You will find meaty texts drawn from sociology, psychology and political thought, organised in ways to produce lively interaction in your classes.

Such 'values clarification' exercises have relevance far beyond language learning, in subjects such as ethics, civilisation and the mother tongue. In fact, much of the material in *The Q Book* is ideal for inter-disciplinary teaching of the sort that is currently becoming popular in places like Spain and Italy, particularly in the last two years of secondary school.

Writing

The last section, 'Students write questionnaires' (pp 105–141) deals both with the learner's attitude to writing (see the introduction to this section, p 105), and with ways in which the learner can be motivated and guided without being put in a straitjacket.

The written activities include a number of paired tasks, to encourage discussion and writing to mix naturally. Writing practice does not have to be a lonely experience; one can work with a partner, write, rethink, rewrite. And all the while, the student knows that what she/he has written will be willingly read by others. In questionnaires, this can be achieved at the sentence level, as a stepping stone to writing paragraphs and more continuous prose.

The teacher's role

Much of the work suggested in this book dispenses with the need for 'frontal teaching'; indeed the most the teacher needs to do in front of the class is to give clear instructions. This frees her/him, particularly in larger classes, for serious work; giving help and advice to individuals, observing the group both as learners and as whole people, and gaining feedback on the effect of the activities. The teacher works more efficiently and the learners learn more. (An excellent compendium of exercises to stop teachers interfering with small-group work is *Sense of Teaching* by Gerry Kenny and Bonnie Tsai, OUP 1989.

During the pair and small-group exercises, there are many exciting things you can do:

– move around quietly acting as a mobile dictionary, feeding words to learners on demand, and/or listening and noting down language errors in preparation for later teaching;

– become a partner in a pair or small group and do the exercise yourself. This brings a number of advantages: you learn a lot about your partner(s); you don't bother other learners; stepping out of the leader role, you perceive the group as a member of it;

– choose a place in the room where you can clearly see a good number of pairs or small groups. Observe your students at work; bodies have a lot to tell about feeling, mood, attitude;

– circulate in the room and listen to the learners' voices, ignoring the semantics of what they are saying. Listen only to tempo, pitch, and voice colouring. Real messages from inside a person are publicly broadcast via her/his voice quality.

A note on affective learning

Some colleagues have felt, in using these exercises, that they were in danger of trespassing on areas that have nothing to do with the classroom, of prying into secret places. We believe this may well be true with some exercises, in some classes, and with some teachers, but that trying to teach a language *without* in some way involving the learner's affective, emotional responses is a poor substitute. It is impossible to predict which exercises will stick in a particular group's gullet, or a particular teacher's gullet. One of the colleagues who piloted *The Q Book* writes: 'There are of course several activities in the book which caused a much less positive, a "wouldn't touch it with a bargepole" reaction in my staffroom. It always fascinates me how my "bargepole" activities are those which other teachers may receive with the greatest enthusiasm, and vice-versa.'

To speak a foreign language fluently the learner has to trust the raft of words he/she is sailing on, and to achieve such trust he/she must have had a chance to say affectively meaningful things in the language. The classroom can be a 'sheltered environment' for new experience; this is why we offer some activities that may well explore areas the learner has not previously thought through in her/his mother tongue. New thinking and new experiences through the target language help to reduce the foreignness of the medium and make the foreign words feel closer, more from within the speaker. This is not to say we dismiss our colleagues' doubts; quite the reverse. To attempt some of the exercises you need to be working with people who know one another reasonably well and are prepared to trust each other and you. This puts demands on the teacher, upon whom the responsibility for achieving group harmony ultimately rests.

It is worth noting, too, that you should be willing to take part in self-disclosure activities if you expect students to do so. It would be odd to ask people in the group to do things you yourself would not feel reasonably able to do. (For an example of a teacher modelling an activity, see 6.17, p 134.) (See Biblio-graphy for books containing 'warm-up' and group dynamic exercises.)

Please do what you like, need or want with these exercises. Following the EFL writers' tradition, we have set out the ideas on the pages of this book as though they were rigid, once-and-for-always lesson plans. They are not. You will obviously remake the exercises you use in the image of your group and to suit yourself. Some of the very best classes come from teachers misunderstanding exercises in books and in so doing, 100% improving them. We are looking forward to being creatively misunderstood.

READING AND DISCUSSION

Section 1

Pairwork questionnaires

This section provides you with a range of questionnaires for your students to work on in pairs. Other sources of questionnaire material include popular magazines, Sunday newspapers, and popular psychological and sociological literature. (A list of useful books is given in the Bibliography, p 142.)

Frequently quoted reasons for finding pairwork useful are:

– vastly increased student talking time
– a chance to experiment fairly privately with the language
– a release for shy students
– a release for the teacher from being permanently centre-stage

If however you propose activities for pairwork that also involve the student in thinking or feeling in new areas, then the student may find out something about both himself/herself and the partner. When enough of this kind of work is done, the foreign language lesson actually becomes a time when a lot more than language is being learnt, just as it was in the process of learning the mother tongue. This has a significant technical benefit; the learner's inner resistance towards the strangeness of the foreign tongue is reduced as it becomes a bearer of important affective learning.

Frequent use of pairwork generates a feeling of mutual supportiveness within the group and teaches the individual to value and rely on not only her/his resources but also on those of partners. One of the curious aspects of the test or exam situation is that precisely this form of mutual help is labelled cheating![1]

[1] Testing of individuals does not inevitably have to work against group values, though. In one school in Japan, students are grouped in threes to prepare for tests, each threesome containing a strong, a weak and an average student. In the test the three work without consultation, and are marked individually, but the final mark given to each is the average of all three. This form of testing fosters collaboration and peer-teaching and would be a marvellous antidote to the divisive way testing is done in most places.

1.1 Time taken

TOPIC
Daily habits

STRUCTURE
How long does/did it take (you) to + infinitive?

LEVEL
Elementary to lower intermediate

TIME
40–55 minutes

MATERIALS
One 'How long?' questionnaire for each pair of students

BACKGROUND
Many students find it helpful to encounter a language structure many times before attempting to use it for themselves. If one wishes to produce a text that is rich in a particular structure, the questionnaire is an ideal medium. The continual repetition of forms and words that would appear strained and artificial in, for example, a coursebook dialogue, is perfectly natural for a questionnaire.

IN CLASS
1 Give one 'How long?' questionnaire to each pair. Student A puts the questions to student B, and then vice versa.

2 Ask each student to write seven *'How long ...'* questions addressed to a friend or family member.

3 Pair the students with the same partners as before. They swap the questionnaires they have each written. So Person A has B's questionnaire and vice-versa. A looks at B and starts asking him/her the questions. B replies in role as the friend or relative (i.e. his/her own friend or relative). They then do the exercise the other way round; B puts to A the questions A wrote and A replies in role as his/her friend or relative.

EXTENSION
Most structures can be used in this type of questionnaire. For example, write, or get your students to write, questionnaires including:

How often do you ...?
Where do you like to ...?
Who do you ... when ...?
How long is it since you + -ed ...?
What would you do if ...?
Do you think you will ever ...?

You will find further structure-rich questionnaires in Section 5: 5.1 Your memory (present simple); 5.4 Ordinary criminality (present perfect).

'How long?' questionnaire

1 How long does it take you to get off to sleep at night?

2 How long does it take you to get up and dressed on a weekday morning?

3 How long did it take you to get up when you were eight or nine?

4 How long does it take you to have a bath or a shower if you are not in a hurry?

5 You are reading an average novel in your own language. How long does it take you to read fifty pages?

6 How long does it take you to eat the main meal of the day?

7 How long did it take you to get from home to school when you were eight?

8 How long does it take you to wash your hair?

9 How long does it take you to make and eat breakfast?

10 How long does it take you to pack for a holiday?

TOPIC
Personal
superlatives
LANGUAGE
The adjective
+ *-est thing*
that ...; present
perfect tense
LEVEL
Elementary to
lower intermediate
TIME
25–40 minutes
MATERIALS
A collection of
very small objects
(tiny toy animals,
seeds, model cars,
things in
matchboxes etc.)
One 'Superlatives'
questionnaire for
each student

1.2 Superlatives

BACKGROUND

The Largest, the Smallest, the Oldest, the Tallest – these fascinate children and adults alike, as is shown by the phenomenal popularity of *The Guinness Book of Records*. This activity links the syntax of superlatives in English to the students' personal experience.

IN CLASS

1 Spread out your collection of small objects on a table and tell the class a short anecdote about some very small thing you possessed when you were young. Alternatively, tell a story based on the following outline:

- a little boy and his father
- at bedtime the boy asks, 'What will you bring me tomorrow?'
- 'A railway engine, a small engine'.
- 'How small? That small?' (show a tiny engine with thumb and forefinger)
- this becomes a ritual; the boy collects everything that is tiny, and keeps them in matchboxes

2 Give one 'Superlatives' questionnaire to each student and ask them to cross out up to ten questions they don't feel like asking. Against each of the remaining questions they should write the name of a fellow student they would like to put that question to. They can put each question to a different person, or all the questions to one person, or any other mix they like.

3 They get up and mill around, putting their questions to each other.

EXTENSION

Ask the students to write their own 'Superlatives' questionnaires.

'Superlatives' questionnaire

1   What is the smallest object you can buy in a supermarket?

2   What is the smallest object you own?

3   What is the oldest possession you have?

4   What is the oldest thing anyone in your family has?

5   What is the smallest thing you have ever bought?

6   What is the largest present you have ever given anyone?

7   Which is the most comfortable chair you have in your home?

8   What is the largest sum of money you have ever carried round on your person?

9   What is the longest meal you have ever eaten?

10   What is the shabbiest thing you own?

11   What is the nicest thing you possess?

12   Which two things would you most want to save if your home caught fire?

13   If you were to burgle your own house, which three things would you take?

14   Which is your strongest leg?

15   What is the smallest thing you have ever seen?

16   What is the shortest book you have read?

17   What is the hottest place you have ever been in?

18   When has your hair been longest?

19   How old is the youngest member of your family?

20   What is the smallest amount you've been paid for an hour's work?

TOPIC Persuasion STRUCTURE *To make/ persuade/get someone to* ... LEVEL Intermediate to upper intermediate TIME 40–55 minutes MATERIALS One 'Who can persuade you?' questionnaire for each pair of students

1.3 Who can persuade you?

BACKGROUND

Most of us would like to believe that we 'make up our own minds' and are not easily 'influenced' by other people, just as we would like to believe that we are honest, truthful, practical, likeable etc. Such beliefs are the very life-blood of the popular questionnaire ...

IN CLASS

1 In pairs A puts the questions to B and vice versa.

2 Ask the students to continue the questionnaires, adding three more situations and three more sets of persuaders.

3 Put the students in fours so they can try their new questions out on each other.

EXTENSION

This exercise can be done with topics other than 'persuasion'. Take 'guilt':

You are involved in a money transaction. The other person gives you too much money and you accept it without telling them about their mistake. In which of these situations would you feel least guilty doing this:

- over a bank counter
- in your wage packet
- paying a parking fine
- receiving a loan repayment from an acquaintance

Take the senses:

You haven't eaten for twenty-four hours and your thoughts are on food. Which of these is more likely to happen:

- you see a mind's eye picture of a dish you hope to have
- an odour wafts into your mental nostrils
- you seem to hear kitchen/dining room sounds
- you feel as though you can taste a certain food
- something else

'Who can persuade you?' questionnaire

1 Imagine you don't feel like wearing your seatbelt. Who would be most successful in getting you to wear it?
   - a police officer ☐
   - a doctor ☐
   - your child ☐
   - your spouse ☐

2 You are waiting to walk across the road. The light is red. You might cross if someone else did first. Whose example would be the strongest?
   - an old lady ☐
   - a child of 10 ☐
   - a smart man of 30 ☐
   - a man of 40 in an oily uniform ☐

3 What is most likely to persuade you to vote a certain way in a general election?
   - fear ☐
   - your parents' example ☐
   - idealism ☐
   - your boss's opinion ☐
   - a party leader's image ☐
   - your spouse's opinion ☐
   - a party's policies ☐

4 Your hobby is gardening. What is most likely to make you change the way you cultivate a certain crop?
   - advice heard on the radio ☐
   - a sudden idea of your own ☐
   - advice read in a newspaper ☐
   - what a friend has told you ☐

5 You spend a lot of time with a selfish friend who monopolises you. Several people tell you not to see the friend so much. Who are you most likely to pay attention to?
   - your mother ☐
   - your boy/girl friend ☐
   - a teacher ☐
   - your father ☐
   - another friend ☐
   - your brother/sister ☐

6 You have a fear of heights. Which of these situations might persuade you to climb a ten-metre ladder?
   - a kitten stuck up a tree ☐
   - a small child stuck up a tree ☐
   - a £1,000 prize ☐
   - rain pouring through your roof ☐
   - people telling you you're a coward ☐

TOPIC Motor accidents LANGUAGE Vocabulary: accident reports; 'interrupted past' (past simple with past continuous) LEVEL Upper intermediate TIME 55–70 minutes MATERIALS One 'Motor accident report' for each student

1.4 Accident

BACKGROUND

This unit is suitable for classes at the upper end of secondary school and for adult groups in car-owning societies. The topic is powerful in two ways; first, in dealing with the car and driving, symbols of emancipation into adulthood, and second, because real accidents are sometimes a life and death area. If people are to learn language to communicate, the things communicated about must have weight and depth.

It is worth bearing in mind that if a person in the group has recently had a serious accident, the exercise may have a relieving and cathartic effect or may be a harrowing reliving of something they would sooner forget. There is no way we, the authors, can predict which. This is where your human, teaching skill lies.

IN CLASS

1 Tell the class the story of a road accident that you or someone close to you has had. Tell the story in detail with a blackboard sketch. This modelling is essential to get students warmed into thinking about their own accident experience.

2 Ask the students to bring back to mind a road accident that they or someone close to them has had and that they remember fairly clearly. If they cannot do this, ask them to invent an accident.

3 Give them the 'Motor accident report' to fill out. You may want to pre-teach some of the vocabulary, e.g. *previous convictions, a prosecution pending, a physical infirmity, policy-holder*. Ask them to fill out the report from a time point about one week after the accident. If the accident is not theirs, tell them to write the report *as* the person who had the accident.

4 Students now tell their accident stories to the class. Supply words they reach out for in the telling and jot these down unobtrusively on the board. Gently facilitate the combined use of past simple and past continuous, where appropriate. (Don't drag the structure in by its hair.)

IN A LATER CLASS

Do a vocabulary revision exercise to recycle the words *needed* by the students in describing their accidents. Give the students a sheet with thirty to forty words on. Ask them to pick out two words they confidently expect to have forgotten by their next birthday, and two they think they will remember. Each student picks these four words working alone.

Divide the board into two areas:

Words to be forgotten   **Words to be remembered**

Students come and write their words on the board.

You now point to words that occur in different handwritings in both areas and ask the writers why they think they will remember/forget them.

Acknowledgement: We learnt this beautiful, paradoxical exercise from Chris Sion. Many more ideas for word revision are to be found in *Vocabulary*, Morgan and Rinvolucri (see Bibliography p. 142).

Note: One of our colleagues opted *not* to use an accident of her own or someone close to her, but played the group a tape in which a person involved in an accident describes it to a policeman. This is a good way of draining the exercise of its human power. Students react to *you* telling *your own* story or the story of someone close to you, your tone of voice, the look on your face, the way you stand or sit. Your students know you – they don't know the scriptwriter or actor who are behind the tape.

PERSON DRIVING OR IN CHARGE OF VEHICLE
(To be completed even if the vehicle was parked)

Name

Address

Date of birth

Occupation (Full and part time)

Employer's name(s)
Tel No(s)

Driving Licence details Number	Date of issue
Whether full or provisional	Country of issue
Vehicle groups	Date driving test passed

Length of driving experience
(i) in this country   (ii) elsewhere

Has the driver been involved in any previous accidents
                    Yes ☐   No ☐
If yes, give details and dates even if previously reported

Has the driver received any previous convictions in respect of motoring offences or has he/she any prosecutions pending   Yes ☐   No ☐
If yes, state date, offence and penalty even if previously reported

Is a prosecution pending as a result of this accident or has a notice of intended prosecution been issued   Yes ☐   No ☐
If yes, give details

Does the driver suffer from any physical infirmity or disease   Yes ☐   No ☐
If yes, give details

Has the driver been refused motor insurance or had special terms imposed on him/her   Yes ☐   No ☐
If yes, give details

State whether the driver is the Policyholder, a relative, friend, colleague, acquaintance or employee

If not the Policyholder, does the driver own a motor vehicle   Yes ☐   No ☐
If yes, state name, address of insurers and policy number

ACCIDENT DETAILS

Location: Street, Town, County

Date	Time	am/pm
Visibility		Daylight, dusk or dark
Weather conditions		Conditions of road surface

What signals did you give

Did you sound your horn Yes ☐ No ☐	Width of road
Street lighting	

What lights were showing on your vehicle

How far was your vehicle from the nearside kerb	What speed limit was in force
Were you on the major road Yes ☐ No ☐	

What was the speed of your vehicle
(i) Before impact   (ii) Upon impact

Was a pedestrian involved   Yes ☐   No ☐
If yes, was he/she on a pedestrian crossing

Give details of any statements of blame made by any person

Whom do you consider responsible for the accident

Did a Police Officer take details of the accident   Yes ☐   No ☐
If yes, state
Number   Station
Name   Police Force

Details of your passengers:
1. Name
   Address
2. Name
   Address

Independent witnesses:
1. Name
   Address
2. Name
   Address

DESCRIPTION OF ACCIDENT

EXPLANATORY SKETCH

Please indicate the insured and all other vehicles involved by their respective registration numbers.

Indicate:
1. The layout of the road
2. The direction of the vehicles
3. Their position at the time of impact
4. The road signs
5. Names of the streets or roads

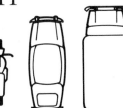 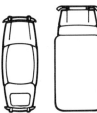

Indicate by an arrow the point of initial impact on the insured vehicle

Indicate by an arrow the point of initial impact on the other vehicle

TOPIC
Personal names

LANGUAGE
Vocabulary:
names (phrases)

LEVEL
Elementary to
advanced

TIME
40–55 minutes

MATERIALS
One 'Names'
questionnaire I for
each pair of
students
One 'Names'
questionnaire II
for each student

1.5 Names

BACKGROUND

A person's name is an important part of self-image. It is also in some ways 'public property', and thus vulnerable, especially in a foreign language context. Questionnaire I looks at one's general perceptions of and feelings about names. Questionnaire II (which is best done in a group that has good internal rapport) explores a little deeper.

IN CLASS

1 Pair the students and ask them to work on 'Names' questionnaire I, A questioning B and then vice versa.

2 Ask pairs to come together in fours to discuss their answers and their feelings towards their names.

3 Ask the students to work alone on 'Names' questionnaire II. Tell them that they may discuss any or all of their answers with others in the group if they wish, but that they don't have to.

Acknowledgement: The questionnaires are based on one in *Active Techniques and Group Psychotherapy*, by Ted Saretsky (Jason Aronson, NY 1977)

'Names' questionnaire I

1   Write 10 English names that you like:

Write your own full name here in block capitals:

....

2   Does your surname have an ordinary meaning in your language (as, for example, the name Butcher in English)?

·3   What is the origin of your surname?

4   Do you know the origin of your personal name(s)?

5   Is the meaning of your name important to you?

6   If you translate your name into English, how does it sound?

7   Do you like to hear other people use your name a lot when talking to you?

8   Do you remember other people's names well?

9   If you had to choose a new name for yourself (e.g. as a pen-name or alias) which name (in your own first language) would you choose?

10   Which English name would you choose?

'Names' questionnaire II

Sign your name here: ....

1 Do you use more than one signature (e.g. one for cheques and one for signing letters)?

2 Do you sign your name slowly or quickly?

3 In what ways does your signature reflect your personality?

4 How do you feel as you sign your name on a cheque, on a job application, on a letter?

5 Do you have strong feelings about anyone else's signature?

6 How many different names do you have, or are you known by? Write some of them here:

7 Is your family name more important to you than your personal name?

8 Have you been given any nicknames within your family? How did they arise?

9 Do you have any other nicknames (e.g. at work, at school)?

10 Have you ever invented a nickname for someone else?

11 What would you feel or what did you feel on changing your name at marriage? Or did you/would you refuse to change your name?

12 In what ways are you like your name?

13 How do you feel when people shorten your name (e.g. Bob for Robert) or expand your name (e.g. Harold for Harry)?

14 Say your name aloud in different ways: whisper it, sing it, pronounce it in a foreign accent, etc.

15 How do you feel when someone misspells or mispronounces your name?

16 Can you think of any ways of improving the spelling or pronunciation of your name?

17 Why did your parents name you as they did?

1.6 Shopping

TOPIC
Personal shopping
habits

LANGUAGE
Present simple
tense + phrases of
time and
frequency

LEVEL
Lower to upper
intermediate

TIME
20–30 minutes

MATERIALS
One 'Shopping'
questionnaire for
each pair of
students
One 'Shopping'
questionnaire
with French
percentages for
each pair of
students

BACKGROUND
In this exercise students are asked to compare their own shopping habits with those of a sample of French people. Statistics from any country could be used but there is no reason why students should restrict their thinking to the UK and the US when using English.

IN CLASS
1 Give out the questionnaire, one to each pair. If your class is a secondary school one, ask the students to answer as the person who actually does the shopping. If it is an adult class, they should obviously answer about their own shopping habits.

2 When the students have asked each other the questions, give them the questionnaire with the French percentages on it. Put them in fours to discuss whether they think these percentages are true of their own country/ies and true of any English-speaking country they know.

Acknowledgement: The original survey, of which this is an adapted version, was carried out by IFRES for *Le Journal du Dimanche* in 1982. They used a sample of 1,000 people.

'Shopping' questionnaire

1 Do you go shopping in a
   supermarket
   Every day it's open ☐
   Several times a week ☐
   Once a week ☐
   Once a month ☐
   Very rarely ☐
   Never? ☐

2 Do you see advantages in buying
   in a supermarket?
   Yes ☐
   No ☐
   Not sure ☐

3 If you answered 'yes' what are the
   advantages you see? (Don't mark
   more than two advantages.)
   Prices normally lower ☐
   Quality of the goods ☐
   Free choice made possible ☐
    by self-service
   No loss of time ☐
   Ease of parking ☐

4 In your case, is going shopping in
   a supermarket
   A bore ☐
   A pleasant outing ☐
   A necessity ☐
   No opinion? ☐

5 You often see special offers in a
   supermarket – do you make a
   beeline for these?
   Yes, always ☐
   Yes, sometimes ☐
   Rarely ☐
   No, never ☐
   No idea ☐

6 Are you loyal to one supermarket
   you like or do you prefer to
   change supermarkets when you
   can?
   I am loyal to one supermarket ☐
   I prefer to change supermarkets ☐
   I don't have the chance to ☐
    change supermarkets
   No feelings on this one ☐

7 In your view, who most usually
   does the family shopping?
   The husband ☐
   The wife ☐
   Both of them together ☐
   The kids ☐
   Someone else ☐

'Shopping' questionnaire with French percentages

A sample of 1,000 people in France were asked these questions and the percentages given on this page show their answers.

1 Do you go shopping in a supermarket

Every day it's open	7%
Several times a week	23%
Once a week	30%
Once a month	20%
Very rarely	16%
Never?	4%

2 Do you see advantages in buying in a supermarket?

Yes	86%
No	8%
Not sure	6%

3 If you answered 'yes' what are the advantages you see? (Don't mark more than two advantages.)

Prices normally lower	69%
Quality of the goods	4%
Free choice made possible by self-service	39%
No loss of time	21%
Ease of parking	19%

4 In your case, is going shopping in a supermarket

A bore	23%
A pleasant moment	19%
A necessity	51%
No opinion?	7%

5 You often seen special offers in a supermarket – do you make a beeline for these?

Yes, always	11%
Yes, sometimes	52%
Rarely	23%
No, never	11%
No idea	3%

6 Are you loyal to one supermarket you like or do you prefer to change supermarkets when you can?

I am loyal to one supermarket	45%
I prefer to change supermarkets	39%
I don't have the chance to change supermarkets	5%
No feelings on this one	11%

7 In your view who most usually does the family shopping?

The husband	7%
The wife	53%
Both of them together	35%
The kids	3%
Someone else	2%

TOPIC Complaining **LANGUAGE** Colloquial vocabulary, e.g. *shoddy, cowboy* etc.; *Is it worth +* gerund; *to go on about* **LEVEL** Upper intermediate **TIME** 15–20 minutes **MATERIALS** One copy of the newspaper article for each student One 'Complaints' questionnaire for each student

1.7 Reading passage to questionnaire

BACKGROUND

Traditionally a reading passage is often a lead-in to question and answer work. Most times the questions are about the overt content of the reading passage. To vary this pattern it is good to sometimes give students a reading passage they work through on their own, without you checking up on them, followed by question/answer work that goes *beyond* the content of the reading.

The technique exemplified in this unit is one you can use with many of the passages in textbooks. A further exercise would be to ask the students to develop their own questionnaires round the theme of a given text. (You could use the text and the new questions in another class!)

IN THE FIRST CLASS

Give the students the article to read for homework.

IN THE SECOND CLASS

1 Pair the students and give out one copy of the 'Complaints' questionnaire to each pair.

2 Ask one person in each pair to put all the questions to the other. When they have finished, ask them to reverse roles.

EXTENSION

- Ask the students to write a letter to the local paper, complaining about some aspect of the school.
- Ask each student to write a dialogue between two people who know him/her well, in which they grouse about the person's habits or behaviour.
- Another useful follow-up to this unit is the Gripes Auction in *Grammar Games*, by Rinvolucri (CUP 1985).
- Write down complaints that were levelled at you in the past by friends, enemies, elders and teachers.

Warning to carpet 'cowboy'

From Our Correspondent
Sheffield

A 'cowboy' carpet fitter has left a trail of complaints in South Yorkshire, and earned the nickname of "Picasso" from consumer protection bodies.

Customers have been so upset after seeing his shoddy workmanship that they have complained in their dozens to the county consumer protection department. On several occasions the complaints have led to civil court actions. But the culprit – whom officials refuse to name – is still weaving his way around the area.

The name Picasso comes from his tendency to leave holes, trying later to fill them with strange shapes.

Among complaints received are that he leaves gaps along walls, has laid a carpet on top of a doorwell with the mat in place, leaving a large hump, and has hacked skirting boards with his knife.

He has also delivered the wrong carpet, and has been known to lay it after the householders, who were away, had left the key with a neighbour. He has delivered carpets to the wrong addresses, and sometimes forgotten who ordered them in the first place.

When customers complain he usually tells them that his van has broken down, and he cannot get there to put matters right.

He has now received a warning from the consumer protection department. Yesterday, Mr Gordon Smith, divisional consumer protection officer, said: 'We have a thick dossier on this man. He is a likable sort of fellow, not an out-and-out rogue, but his idea of conducting his business is very poor.

'He is very well known to us through the complaints we have had over a number of years.'

A spokesman for the British Standards Institute said that a new code of practice had been drawn up, covering domestic carpet-fitting, which was now being circulated.

THE TIMES 16.2.83

'Complaints' questionnaire

1 What would you do if someone did work as badly as this carpet fitter in your house or flat?

2 Can you think of other people in your family or your circle of friends who might react differently from you in the carpet fitter situation?

3 Have you or your parents ever had to complain about bad work done in your house or flat or to your car?

4 Were such complaints successful?

5 Do you personally like complaining?

6 Do/did teachers at school complain about your work?

7 If so, how do/did they complain: orally; in writing to you; to the head of the school; to your parents?

8 Did teachers ever threaten you? If so what with?

9 Did teachers ever carry out their threats? How did you feel?

10 Who, in your life, has complained most about you? What about, mainly?

11 Who or what have you complained about most in your life?

12 Is complaining useful? If so, who to and why?

13 Is complaining an excessive need in some people? Do you know someone like this? If yes, describe him/her.

14 Do people tend to complain more when someone from outside the family comes to stay or live in their house?

15 Do old people complain more than younger people? Give examples.

16 Do people complain about police behaviour in your country? What sort of things?

17 Is it worth a child complaining about his/her parents and brothers and sisters? Did you ever?

18 Is it worth parents complaining about their kids' behaviour? Do you know of instances of this?

19 If A does something bad to you, is it worth moaning to B about it? Do you do a lot of indirect complaining?

20 Do you know any hypochondriacs? What sort of things do they go on about?

TOPIC
Gadgets you like

LANGUAGE
*Would you prefer
to ...?*

LEVEL
Intermediate

TIME
20–40 minutes

MATERIALS
One 'Technical
choice'
questionnaire for
each pair of
students

1.8 Technical choice

BACKGROUND
'Let's talk about something interesting!' very often means 'Let's talk about me!'
Many conversations, and most popular questionnaires, work on this principle.

IN CLASS
1 Pair the students and give each pair a copy of the questionnaire.

2 Ask the members of each pair to put the questions to each other alternately.

3 Ask each pair to write five to ten more questions of a similar type and then
  to exchange questions with the neighbouring pair. In some classes this will
  lead into a general discussion of technology in one's personal life.

'Technical choice' questionnaire

1 Would you light a cigarette with a match or a lighter?

2 Would you prefer to use a hand whisk or an electric mixer to prepare an omelette?

3 Would you write a letter to a friend on a typewriter or with a pen?

4 Would you check your shopping bill with pen and paper or with a pocket calculator?

5 Do you prefer going to the cashier to cash a cheque or getting the money from an automatic cash dispenser?

6 You have pulled up at a garage for petrol. Are you disappointed or not to find that it's a self-service pump?

7 Would you prefer to ring someone up on a traditional telephone or a videophone?

8 Given enough money, would you buy a luxury car or a helicopter?

9 Would you open a bottle of wine with a corkscrew or a special cork extractor?

10 If you have to make a journey of 500 km, would you prefer to go by rail or air?

TOPIC Cinema and TV; the older generations LANGUAGE Expressing approval, disapproval, censure; motivated intensive reading LEVEL Upper intermediate to advanced TIME 55–70 minutes MATERIALS One 'Cinema attitudes' questionnaire for each student

1.9 Grandparents

BACKGROUND

This activity is aimed particularly at teenagers and younger adults. It uses the technique of doubling or role-empathy to widen the field of discussion and to throw unexpected light on the students' own feelings about both the topic and the older generations.

The questionnaire is in the form of a series of statements to be rated on an agree/disagree scale. For this reason, some of the statements may appear at first glance very similar to each other; only on close reading will the differences emerge.

IN CLASS

1 Ask each student to write a paragraph describing the room or place in which they normally see or saw *one* of their grandparents. If anybody cannot, or would prefer not to, remember a grandparent, ask them to choose someone else they know or knew well of the same generation. (Visualising a *place* associated with a person is for many people a powerful way of evoking that person.)

2 In pairs, the students read their paragraphs to each other and explain further about the place or room.

3 Ask the students to try and bring to mind a couple of things the grandparent or old person would habitually say and the sort of voice they spoke in. Ask them to exchange this information with their partners.

4 Give each student a copy of the 'Cinema attitudes' questionnaire. Explain that these were statements collected in the pre-World War II period when cinema was young and there was no TV. Ask them to think of their grandparent and to write 0 against any statement he/she would have totally agreed with, and 5 against any statement he/she would have totally disagreed with. They should then mark 1, 2, 3 or 4 to show intermediate attitudes.

5 Ask pairs of students to come together in fours to compare their grandparents' attitudes to the cinema.

6 Ask the students individually to write down five sentences to express what their grandparent feels or would have felt about present-day TV.

7 In the same fours they compare grandparental attitudes to TV.

'Cinema attitudes' questionnaire

The following statements are a few out of more than 200 collected by L.L. Thurstone in 1930.

Think of an old person that you know quite well, for example, a grandparent or neighbour. Which of the following statements on the cinema would he/she agree with? In the space provided, write 0 against any statement he/she would have totally agreed with at that time and 5 against any statement they would have totally disagreed with. Put 1, 2, 3 or 4 to show intermediate attitudes.

1 Going to the cinema occupies time that should be spent in more wholesome recreation. ☐

2 I am tired of films – I have seen too many poor ones. ☐

3 The cinema is the best civilising device ever developed. ☐

4 Films are the most important cause of crime. ☐

5 Films are all right but a few give the rest a bad name. ☐

6 I like to see films once in a while, but they do disappoint you sometimes. ☐

7 I think films are fairly interesting. ☐

8 Films are just a harmless pastime. ☐

9 Going to the cinema to me is just a way to kill time. ☐

10 The influence of the cinema is decidedly for good. ☐

11 Films are good clean entertainment. ☐

12 Films increase one's appreciation of beauty. ☐

13 I'd never miss the cinema if we didn't have it. ☐

14 It is a sin to go to the cinema. ☐

15 There would be very little progress without the cinema. ☐

16 Films are the most vital form of art today. ☐

17 A film once in a while is a good thing for everybody. ☐

18 A film once in a while is one of the few good things I can enjoy by myself. ☐

19 Films are wholly bad for children. ☐

20 I like to see other people enjoy films, whether I enjoy them myself or not. ☐

21 Films are to blame for the increase in sexual offences. ☐

22 The cinema is one of the great educational institutions for the common people. ☐

23 Young people are learning to smoke and pet from films. ☐

24 The cinema is the best cheap entertainment. ☐

25 Films are undermining respect for authority. ☐

Now write ten or so statements that people of your parents' generation might agree with.

TOPIC
Life-style at fourteen

1.10 Sweet fourteen

TOPIC
Life-style at
fourteen

LANGUAGE
Present simple
tense

LEVEL
Elementary to
intermediate

TIME
30–45 minutes

MATERIALS
One 'Fourteen-
year-old'
questionnaire for
each student

BACKGROUND

This is a silent reading exercise to be done by people of sixteen and up. The questionnaire was originally designed to be answered by fourteen-year-olds, but here we propose it as a time-travel reading role-play. The students are invited to answer the questions from the standpoint of when they were fourteen. Steps 1 to 3 are aimed at helping them to return to that age, mentally and imaginatively.

IN PREVIOUS CLASS

Ask any students who can to bring photos of themselves at 14 years old.

IN CLASS

1 Ask those who have brought photos of themselves to show these round the class.

2 Ask each person to tell his/her neighbour three things that happened to him/her in their fourteenth year.

3 Ask people to describe to their neighbours how they wore their hair then.

4 Give each student a questionnaire to read and respond to (by ticks and in writing).

5 Ask the students to form pairs and to look through each other's answers, asking questions and commenting where they want to. Quite a lot of paired discussion normally ensues.

6 A good way of rounding off this unit is by asking the group what has changed for fourteen-year-olds since their day. Ask how many people have siblings of thirteen to fifteen. Ask them to tell everybody how things are different for these siblings, compared with what they themselves experienced at that age. Areas to explore could include sexual behaviour, relations with parents, attitudes towards food, money, ambitions, etc.

'Fourteen-year-old' questionnaire

First please tell us a little bit about yourself – **remember you are now 14**.

1   a) How many brothers and sisters have you altogether?   ....

    b) If you have any brothers and sisters
       i) How many of them are older than you are?   ....
      ii) How many of them are younger than you are?   ....

2   Describe carefully the sort of job you would like to do when you leave school. Remember you are now 14.

....

....

....

3   Now, what is the name of your mother's job and your father's job?

....

....

....

Describe carefully the sort of work each does.

....

....

....

4   Below is a list of things that children sometimes do in their spare time after school. Tick the three things you like doing best.

Sports and games   □
Cycling with a group of boys/girls   □
Going to the cinema   □
Going dancing   □
Reading, writing or drawing   □
Woodwork or making models and other things   □
Watching TV or listening to the radio   □
Gardening or care of pets   □
Going to coffee bars   □
Going to youth clubs   □
Going out with boys/girls   □
Chatting to a group of friends   □

5   Do you spend most of your spare time at home or do you mostly go out?
Tick one.

Mostly at home   □
Mostly out   □
Half and half   □

(continued . . .)

6 Do you like spending time on your own or do you prefer to be with other teenagers?
   Tick one.

   I like to be on my own   ☐
   I like to be with other teenagers   ☐
   I don't care   ☐

7 Do you often feel bored because you have nothing to do in your spare time? Tick one.

   I am often bored   ☐
   I am sometimes bored   ☐
   I am seldom or never bored   ☐

8 Do you play for your Form or for your School or Club in any sports?
   Yes   ☐
   No   ☐

9 Which of these do you like best? Tick one.

   To read a story or see a film or TV programme
      about young people at school   ☐
   To read a story or see a film or TV programme
      about young people in their spare time   ☐
   To read a story or see a film or TV programme
      about young people at work   ☐

10 With whom do you mostly go out? Tick one.

    With a boy friend   ☐
    With a group of boys   ☐
    With a group of girls   ☐
    With a group of boys and girls   ☐
    Alone   ☐
    With a girl friend   ☐
    With adults   ☐

11 Some children smoke cigarettes while they are still at school. Have you ever tried smoking a
    cigarette?

    Yes   ☐
    No   ☐

12 Have you smoked more than one cigarette?

    Yes   ☐
    No   ☐

13 a) How many children are there in your form at school? ....
    b) What position would you say you hold in your form in general, that is, taking account of
       all the school subjects? Tick one.

    In the top five   ☐
    In the top ten   ☐
    Just above the middle   ☐
    Below the middle   ☐

14 a) How much money do you have altogether each week that you can save or spend in any
       way you like?
       Write down the approximate amount here: ....
    b) Do you save any of this money?

(continued . . .)

Yes ☐
No ☐

If Yes, what are you saving up for? Tick one

To buy records ☐
To buy a record player or tape recorder or radio ☐
To buy a musical instrument ☐
To buy clothes ☐
To buy sports equipment ☐
To buy books ☐
To buy a bicycle or bicycle spare parts ☐
For a holiday ☐
Something else ☐

15 Do you do any paid job outside school hours?
Yes ☐
No ☐

16 Are you usually broke at the end of the week?
Yes ☐
No ☐

17 If you had enough money, in which of these ways would you like to spend it? Tick each one either Yes or No.

	Yes	No
a) Buy records	☐	☐
b) Buy a record player or tape recorder or radio		
c) Buy a musical instrument	☐	☐
d) Buy clothes	☐	☐
e) Buy sports equipment	☐	☐
f) Buy books	☐	☐
g) Buy cigarettes	☐	☐
h) Buy sweets or ice cream	☐	☐
i) Buy a bicycle or bicycle spare parts		
j) Take a holiday or travel	☐	☐
k) . . .	☐	☐

18 a) Do you ever feel nervous or tense? Tick one.

Often ☐
Sometimes ☐
Hardly ever ☐

b) When you do feel nervous or tense do you do any of these things to help you relax? Tick each one either Yes or No.

	Yes	No
i) Bite your nails	☐	☐
ii) Chew gum	☐	☐
iii) Read a comic	☐	☐
iv) Smoke a cigarette	☐	☐
v) Chew a pencil	☐	☐

TOPIC
Who may ask which questions?

LANGUAGE
Interrogative forms of all kinds

LEVEL
Intermediate to advanced

TIME
45–60 minutes

MATERIALS
One 'Right to ask' questionnaire for each student

1.11 The right to ask

BACKGROUND

Question-and-answer situations occur throughout one's life. The relationship of questioner to answerer, and the right to ask specific questions, vary according to situation. In this activity, students are invited simultaneously to practise question forms and to question the legitimacy of the questions asked.

IN CLASS

1 Give out one copy of the 'Right to ask' questionnaire to each student and explain the instructions if necessary. Each student should work alone on his/her questionnaire.

2 Put the students together in fours to discuss their judgements about who has the right to ask what.

3 Ask the fours to think about this situation:

A couple who cannot have children are thinking of taking on a surrogate mother. An egg taken from the wife and fertilised with the husband's sperm will be implanted in the surrogate's womb. She will carry the child, be delivered of it and give it to the couple. For this service she will be paid.

Ask half the fours to work out a set of fifteen questions the couple will want to ask the surrogate before entering into an agreement with her.
The other half of the fours work out a set of fifteen questions the woman will want to ask the couple.

4 Pair the fours so that they can discuss the problem of surrogate motherhood from both angles.

'Right to ask' questionnaire

For each question, put a tick in column A, B, C and/or D if you think it would be acceptable if asked by

    A   an employer at a job interview
    B   a priest in an interview prior to his accepting you into his religion
    C   a lawyer, before taking on your defence in a criminal case
    D   a life insurance representative who is writing a policy for you

		A	B	C	D
1	What is the main problem facing you at the moment?				
2	When were you born?				
3	Where were you born?				
4	How old were your parents when you were born?				
5	Were you conceived in wedlock?				
6	What are/were your parents' occupations?				
7	Do you have any brothers or sisters?				
8	What jobs do your brother(s) and sister(s) do?				
9	Are you married?				
10	If you are married, what is your wife/husband's occupation?				
11	If you have a child, how long after the date of your marriage was it born?				
12	Was your first child conceived before or after marriage?				
13	How did you feel about your first pregnancy?				
14	What is your present job?				
15	Are you happy in your job?				
16	How much money do you earn?				
17	What were your best subjects at school?				
18	Did you love your parents when you were a child?				
19	What examinations have you passed?				
20	At what age did you leave school?				
21	Are you now, or have you at any time been, a member of the Communist Party?				
22	How many and what jobs have you done?				
23	Which was your longest term of employment, and which the shortest?				
24	Have you ever been sacked from a job?				
25	If so, why?				
26	Do you smoke? If so, how much per week?				
27	Do you drink? Please quantify.				
28	Have you ever taken drugs other than for medical reasons?				
29	Have you ever had a serious illness? If so, give full details.				
30	Have you ever been in trouble with the police?				
31	Have you ever been convicted of a crime?				
32	If you are married, have you ever been unfaithful to your spouse?				
33	To your knowledge, has your spouse ever been unfaithful to you?				
34	Have you ever had a homosexual affair?				
35	What is the worst thing that has ever happened to you?				
36	What is the best thing that has ever happened to you?				
37	What has made you most angry in your life?				
38	Have you ever changed your religion?				
39	Would you say that you are a violent person?				
40	Have you or your family ever suffered from mental illness?				

TOPIC
Various

LANGUAGE
Interrogative
forms of all kinds;
vocabulary: daily
life

LEVEL
Elementary to
advanced

TIME
20–30 minutes
(each)

MATERIALS
One copy of
each questionnaire
for each pair of
students

1.12 Mini-questionnaires

BACKGROUND

Conversations and interviews between people in class, especially between people who know each other quite well, can easily become desultory and unmemorable if they have no structure, but stilted and mechanical if the structure is too rigid (e.g. 'four-line dialogues'). Constructing an oral questionnaire on a theme that is slightly off-centre is one way of giving structure without predictability to a classroom interaction. Such 'mini-questionnaires' can be used in the way a TV interviewer feeds questions to the interviewee.

IN CLASS

Choose, or ask the students to choose, well-defined but less obvious themes for the mini-questionnaire. Some examples of themes are given. Working alone, each student should write five to eight questions on the theme which they will then put to one or more other students orally. Then, in pairs or groups of three or four, the students ask each other the questions they have prepared. Encourage them to put supplementary or 'follow-up' questions whenever an answer suggests further questioning.

Depending on the language level and general experience of the class, the teacher may 'model' part of a mini-questionnaire at the start of the exercise, or suggest two or three questions just to start people's imagination working.

Further themes: tidiness; regular but arbitrary routines; preparations for a journey; things you do on trains; sleep; your memory; silly things that make you angry; when, where, how you watch TV, . . .

Example themes and questions

Getting dressed

When you get dressed in the morning:

1   Is the order in which you put your clothes on important to you?
2   Do you usually dress in your bedroom, in the bathroom, or in some other place?
3   Do you choose what to wear in the morning or the previous day?
4   Do you dress before breakfast or after?
5   . . . . . .

The telephone

1   Where do you make most of your telephone calls?
2   Do you make or receive most of your calls?
3   Do you have a preferred way of standing/sitting when on the telephone?
4   At the end of a telephone call, is it usually you or the other person who ends the call?
5   What would be the average length of your telephone calls?
6   Are there people whom you prefer to talk to on the telephone rather than face to face?
7   . . . . . .

Delaying

1   Do you generally arrive early/just on time/a bit late/half an hour late for a film?
2   Which regular tasks do you generally delay doing?
3   Who is the worst delayer among your family and friends? Why?
4   How do you feel if a train/bus is delayed?
5   When was the last time you kept someone waiting? What happened?
6   When was the last time someone kept you waiting? What happened?
7   . . . . . .

Tête-à-tête

When you are sitting and talking with one other person:

1   Do you prefer to sit next to them, or face to face?
2   Do you generally sit forward in the chair, or lean back?
3   How close to your partner do you like to sit? Does this vary according to who you're talking to?
4   Do you like to have something in your hands (e.g. a pen, a cup, a bracelet, a cigarette) to play with while talking?
5   . . . . . .

Hands

1   When do you keep your hands in your pockets? While standing doing nothing? While walking? While sitting?
2   In English we say, 'To know something as well as the back of one's hand'. Close your eyes and describe the back of your hand.
3   Do you ever try to tell the age of someone from their hands?
4   How do you clap?
5   Are there ways in which you would like to change your hands?
6   Can you do any special tricks with your hands, e.g. click the joints, move all the fingers independently, bend your thumb back to touch your wrist?
7   . . . . . .

READING AND DISCUSSION

Section 2

Quizzes

Quizzes tempt one in many ways: as competitions, against others or oneself; as indicators of the knowledge expected of one by society or fashion, as entertainment; as a painless way of absorbing new knowledge; and as a means of questioning one's assumptions.

The activities in this section exploit all these features to provide motivated reading practice in quiz form.

TOPIC
Making sense
of perception

LANGUAGE
Wh-questions

LEVEL
Lower to middle
intermediate

TIME
35–50 minutes

MATERIALS
One 'Sensation
quiz' sheet for
each pair
One 'Possible
answers' sheet
for each pair

2.1 Sensations

BACKGROUND

Students are generally rather puzzled/annoyed when they start doing this
exercise. They find the questions odd. This is excellent in terms of reading;
they really have to check they *do* understand, rather than just feel happy with
getting the general drift.

Gradually students find that they *can* find satisfactory answers to some of
the questions. Their interest begins to rise:

When you give out the 'Possible answers' they normally become fully
animated and start trying to match questions to answers. This provokes a lot
of detailed reading and re-reading.

You have here a very intensive reading exercise that plunges most students
into a state of frustration at the beginning and then releases them into a
state of high energy. The emotional design of the exercise has much in
common with frustration/release exercises in drama training.

IN CLASS

1 To lead into the questionnaire show a picture out-of-focus on the OHP or on
  a slide projector. Get the students guessing as you slowly bring the picture
  into focus.

2 Give out the quiz sheet and ask the students, in pairs, to answer the
  questions, working together.

3 Give out the possible answer sheet and ask them to match the answers to
  the questions. (The answers are not in the same order as the questions.)
  Make it clear to the students that some of their answers may well be *better*
  than those given on the answer sheet.

Note: One of the teachers who piloted this book writes about this exercise:

'I explained to students beforehand that they might find this exercise frustrating
at first, and that seemed to set a positive mood. They all said they enjoyed
working the questions out and really enjoyed the discussion on perception which
ensued. It led on to a couple more perception exercises. So it was more interesting and
fun than I originally thought and than the notes had led me to believe. Good
vocabulary and reading work as well.'

'Sensation quiz' sheet

1   When is your fist a lot larger than your head?

2   What part of you is shorter in the tropics than in a country like New Zealand or England?

3   In what everyday situation does the hair on your arm stick up?

4   When do some people think they're flying unaided through the air?

5   When can you see something that's not actually there?

6   When are you unsure whether she is old or young?

7   When do you manage to see two people, though there is only one there?

8   Where are you if, as you eat your lunch, your steak floats off?

9   If you can see a part of the world looking like a relief map, where are you?

10 When do you think you are going fairly slowly, though in fact you are still moving pretty fast?

11 What part of you grows and shrinks as you go down a street at night?

12 What are you if you have to wait for a sound before you cross the road?

13 When does everything you can see seem to be spinning round?

14 When is it hard to tell a duck from a rabbit?

15 When does an elephant look bigger than a church?

16 Where are you if you think you are moving gradually faster, though in fact you are stationary?

17 When do you feel that you are getting heavier and heavier?

'Possible answers' sheet

(Some questions have more than one answer. The possible answers are not in the same order as the questions.)

- When it is close to you and the building is far away
- In dreams
- Looking from the window of an aircraft
- When the church is a model
- In a train, watching another train pull out of a station
- In this picture:

- On re-entry from space
- When you have just come off the motorway
- Your shadow
- After drinking too much
- When you have just rolled down a grassy bank
- Blind
- When reflected in the side of a shiny teapot
- In this picture:

- In trick photographs
- In the bath with the water running out round you
- When you shut your eyes tightly and the vision of something seen recently comes back
- When you hallucinate
- On re-entry from space
- When you take off a synthetic blouse or shirt

TOPIC
The news

LANGUAGE
Journalistic
writing; scanning

LEVEL
Upper
intermediate to
advanced

TIME
20–30 minutes

MATERIALS
One copy of a
complete
newspaper page
for each team
A different set of
six questions for
each team, based
on the newspaper
page (the
reproduced page
and questions
shown are samples
of the kinds of
questions you can
put to students
from a variety of
articles, including
advertisements
and photographs)

2.2 Fast reading

BACKGROUND

While Sensations (2.1) is a good example of an intensive reading exercise, the newspaper work below is designed to help students retrieve specific bits of information from a long text. It trains them to swoop on what is relevant, ignoring the rest.

The exercise is particularly useful if you have a mixed ability class. If you have a few students who are a lot less good than the rest, give them the set of questions that are *most difficult* to answer. In step 2 below, you help them find the answers to their questions. This puts them in a position of power during step 3, when they watch the stronger students sweating to answer their questions.

You may wonder why the students are asked to stand round a newspaper page stuck to a wall. This is for a number of reasons:
– learners spend much too much time seated, so standing is a relief
– when four people are standing round their page of the newspaper at the wall they are mobile, they can quickly go from finger-pointing reading to swinging round to face other groups
– standing raises the aggression level and this is a highly competitive activity (we feel the aggression is technically justified in that it ensures high speed reading)

Since students don't usually whisper their answers, in step 3 you should warn colleagues either side of your classroom that this lesson could be a noisy one!

IN CLASS

1 Divide your class into four teams, A, B, C and D. Give one copy of the newspaper page and one set of questions to each team.

2 Ask the teams to stick their pages and questions on the wall and to quickly check the answers to their set of questions. Ask them to note down the answers, as they will be quiz-masters in the next stage of the activity.

3 You are now ready to start the quiz.
Ask team A to read out their first question as loudly and clearly as they can. The other teams have to find the answer from their newspaper page as fast as they can. (Each team has the *same* page.) Team A is responsible for telling you who to give a point to. They have to decide which team out of B, C and D a) gets their answer in first b) offers an adequate answer.
Team B now become quiz-master and read out their first question. C, D, and A have to find the answer as fast as they can.
Apart from learning to scan and read, the learners are also learning to speak loudly and clearly and to listen to each other, despite the competitive excitement.

VARIATION

Once you have played the fast-reading quiz a couple of times you can have the students themselves prepare their own questions. To ensure that the questions set are not too hard, thus defeating the speed reading aim, make it clear that questions written by Team A will be asked by Team B, with Teams C and D competing to answer and so on.

Acknowledgement: We learnt this exercise from *Action speaks Louder, A Handbook of Nonverbal Techniques,* by Jane Remocker and Elizabeth Storch (Churchill Livingstone 1979). There are plenty of useful language exercises in this therapy-focussed book.

Philippine army and guerrillas clash in weekend of violence

Manila: Philippine troops and Communist rebels clashed yesterday about 30 miles north of the capital, with at least three government soldiers killed and two wounded.

Local police contacted by telephone said the gunbattle in Bulacan province between army troops backed by helicopters and guerrillas began in the morning and continued through much of the day. They could not say if the rebels had also suffered casualties.

The Bulacan fighting coincided with an army offensive in the Bicol region, where fresh troops and several armoured personnel carriers were airlifted in yesterday to pursue an estimated 500 Communist New People's Army (NPA) rebels blamed for blowing up five bridges in the area this month.

The troops were believed to be reinforcing the elite Scout Ranger battalion flown into the agricultural region 150 miles south-east of the capital three days ago.

Army Rangers overran an NPA camp in Camarines Sur province on Saturday but the brief gun-battle caused no casualties, army reports said.

The military said the rebels, in blowing up vital road and rail links in Bicol, apparently wanted to isolate the region and divert troops from other areas, clearing the way for attacks on army positions.

A small explosion was reported yesterday at the headquarters of the Philippine Constabulary, the military's internal security force. The blast, in an outdoor rubbish container, caused minor damage but no injuries. The cause of the explosion was unknown.

It was also reported that rebels had blown up power transformers in Aklan province, central Philippines, plunging several villages into darkness.

In Manila, a prominent leftwinger said yesterday that President Corazon Aquino's only chance of remaining in office lay in a power-sharing agreement with the country's rightwing forces. But he did not predict whether her partners would be politicians or the staunchly anti-Communist army.

"On the assumption that there will be no dramatic introduction of new forces, the only way she can last is to accept a power-sharing formula with the Right," Mr Edicio de la Torre, a Roman Catholic priest and head of a leftwing research unit called the Institute of Popular Democracy, said in an interview with the Manila Chronicle newspaper.

He ruled out any "dramatic introduction of new forces" in the form of an early attempt by the Left to seize power.

Mr de la Torre, who was gaoled during the regime of the former President, Mr Ferdinand Marcos, for alleged links with Communists, predicted such an alliance could be forged within a year. He said the alternative to power sharing would be a permanently unstable Government.

Mrs Aquino has been under tremendous public pressure to restore political stability in a country racked by at least five coup attempts in the past year. She is also grappling with a growing Communist insurgency.

● Senior Philippine government officials have been ordered to return Mercedes-Benz limousines lent to them earlier this year as perks of their office, the new customs commissioner announced this weekend. — Reuter.

Prison denial

From Jasper Becker in Peking

A SENIOR official has scoffed at allegations that Tibet has 80 gaols holding thousands of prisoners.

Tibet has only one prison and two labour camps with 974 inmates, Mr Zicheng, president of the Tibet Autonomous Region's Higher People's Court, told the New China News Agency.

More than 20 Tibetans now being held are held on counter-revolutionary charges while 97 per cent were convicted on criminal charges, he said. During the 1983 crackdown on crime in China, 16 people, including 11 Tibetans, were executed for rape, looting and murder.

Last week the New China News Agency criticised the visit to the United States of the Dalai Lama, Tibet's exiled spiritual leader who fled to India in 1959 with 100,000 followers.

The Chinese Government has invited the Dalai Lama to return on condition that he reside in Peking. Negotiations started in 1977 have broken down.

Team A's questions

1   What have Philippine government officials been asked to return?
2   What do you need to read things written with a Berol pen?
etc.

Team B's questions

1   Which country has the Dalai Lama recently visited?
2   How many bridges are the NPA said to have blown up this month in Bicol?
etc.

Team C's questions

1   What did the rebels blow up in Aklan province?
2   When did the Dalai Lama flee to India?
etc.

Team D's questions

1   Who is offering home insurance?
2   How many coup attempts have there been against Mrs Aquino during the last year?
etc.

TOPIC
Countries

LANGUAGE
Vocabulary: simple
geography

LEVEL
Post-beginner to
intermediate

TIME
20–30 minutes

MATERIALS
One copy of the
country outlines
for each pair of
students.

2.3 Geography quiz

IN CLASS

1 Give each pair a copy of the shapes on the opposite page. Ask them to decide which countries are represented. Tell them:
   - not all six countries are drawn to the same scale
   - the dot within each country represents the political capital
   - not all the countries are aligned on the page as you would see them on a conventional atlas page

2 Ask them to write ten to fifteen questions about the geography of *one* of the countries. The pairs work together on this. Here are a couple of example questions about Norway:

How many people live North of the Arctic Circle?
How many countries border on Norway?

We suggest you *don't* give the class examples – let them ask what *they* want, untrammelled.

3 The pairs then form fours and try their quizzes out on each other.

4 Get three or four people who like geography to collect in the questions no one can answer. They do a bit of research and present this to the class in the next lesson.

VARIATION

In a multi-national class you might want to use outlines of the countries the different students come from. You would not want to give a student her/his own country, as far as possible.

Acknowledgement: The idea of getting students to identify the shapes of countries taken out of context we got from Lou Spaventa. Here it is used as a lead-in to getting people to think in spatial, geographical terms.
   The countries are: Spain, the USA, France, Eire, Norway and India.

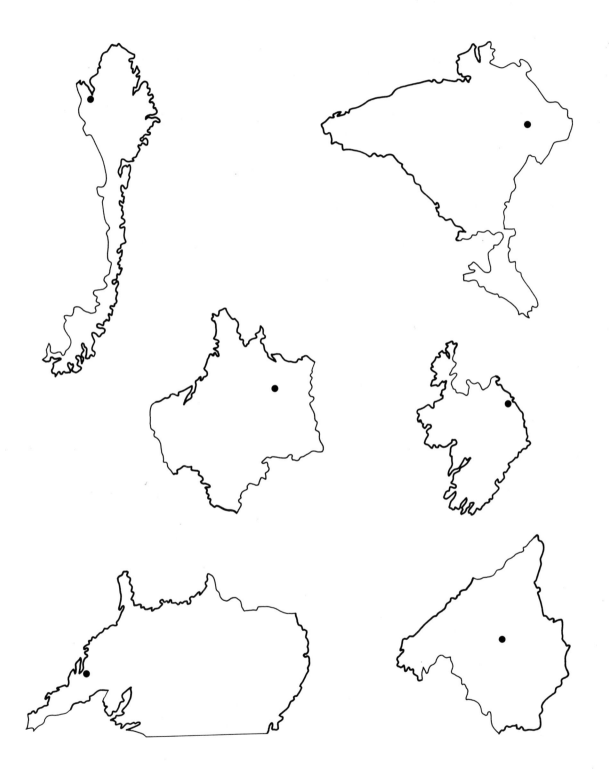

TOPIC Relationship between tramps and society LANGUAGE Free discussion LEVEL Elementary to intermediate TIME 20–30 minutes MATERIALS One 'Tramp signs' quiz for each pair of students One key for each pair of students

2.4 Tramp signs

BACKGROUND

To give the students a feel for how this special sub-cultural sign system works we offer five examples of signs and their meanings. This allows the student to enter the tramp's world a little bit.

The important thing about the tramp signs is the speculation they provoke from your students, not how many signs they guess 'correctly'. In fact, people learn quite a lot about each other when they listen to the revealing things their classmates say about marginalised people like tramps.

IN CLASS

1 Tell an anecdote or incident you know about a tramp. See if there are other stories like this around in the group.

2 Ask the students to work in pairs giving their answers to the 'Tramp signs' quiz.

3 Get the pairs to form fours and compare their ideas.

4 Give out the key for people to check their answers against the meanings assigned by tramps themselves.

5 Ask the students to invent more signs for things tramps might want to say to each other.

EXTENSION

When the class has completed the exercise, ask them to think of other groups of people who might find it useful to invent symbol languages for themselves, and to suggest some of the symbols they might use. (Examples: building workers, policemen, stockbrokers, students)

Acknowledgement: The tramp signs were taken from *Shepherd's Glossary of Graphic Signs and Symbols*, by Walter Shepherd (Dent 1971).

'Tramp signs' quiz

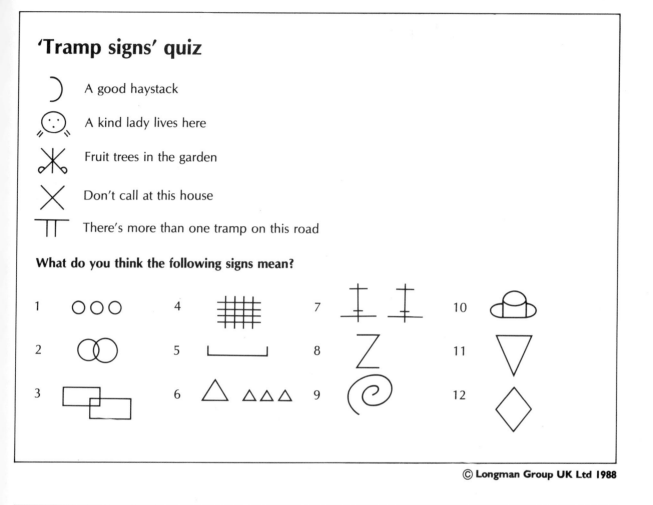

What do you think the following signs mean?

© Longman Group UK Ltd 1988

The key

1 Money usually given here

2 Tell the people in this house a pathetic story

3 The people here are afraid of tramps

4 Get away quickly – ex-prison-warder lives here

5 Invalids – be sympathetic

6 Woman with children – spin a tale about own children

7 People here will telephone the police

8 A foreigner lives here – tell an ex-army story

9 A good workhouse

10 Policeman's house

11 Spoilt – too many callers

12 Generous people but don't press for too much

© Longman Group UK Ltd 1988

READING AND DISCUSSION

Section 3

Values

Our values – moral, social, material – underlie much of what we say and do, but are often deeply hidden, even to ourselves. The activities in this section use a variety of techniques (questionnaire, rank-ordering, forced choice and so on) designed to clarify and make explicit the hidden value systems we each possess.

For the language learner these activities provide more than 'content' to reading and speaking practice. They give the learner an opportunity to experience and discover something new – about themselves or others – through the target language. In this way the language learnt becomes part of the learner's personal development, as the mother tongue was.

<table>
<tr><td>

TOPIC
Information
protection

LANGUAGE
Present simple
tense

LEVEL
Intermediate to
advanced

TIME
30–45 minutes

MATERIALS
One 'Census
questions' sheet
for each pair of
students

</td></tr>
</table>

3.1 The census

BACKGROUND

This is one of a number of exercises in the book which invite students to cross out sentences they find inappropriate. This exercise type is powerful especially with adolescents.

When first done, this kind of exercise has a shock effect, as the student is not often asked to put lines through text given out by a teacher. (We first used the idea in 'Revenge Questions', a unit in *Once Upon a Time*, by Morgan and Rinvolucri (CUP 1984).)

IN CLASS

1 Ask the group a few introductory questions around the census, e.g.
   - Can you remember a census being taken?
   - Which day of the week is it done on?
   - Why does the Government need to take censuses?
   - Are there some people who disagree with having to answer certain questions?
   - Which type of questions?

2 Pair the students and tell them they are part of a committee whose job it is to approve or throw out a new set of census questions. Ask them to work their way through the questions, crossing out the ones they feel should not be asked, and adding new ones as they see fit.

3 Ask the students to put their names on their edited 'Census questions'. Stick these up around the walls of the room and ask people to look at each other's. This will often generate fluid, small-group discussion.

Census questions

(In a real census, failing to answer questions or answering falsely carries a prison sentence.)

1   What is your address?

2   What is your phone number?

3   What is your social security number?

4   Do you own a car?

5   If you answered 'Yes' to No. 4, what is your vehicle registration number?

6   Do you own the place you live in?

7   Would you classify the place you live in as:

    a house   a flat   a mansion   a palace   a bed-sitter   a shanty   a tent

8   How many toilets are there in your residence?

9   How many bedrooms are there in the place you live in?

10   How many children have you got?

11   How many children do you plan to have?

12   Are you married/single/separated/divorced/bigamously married/polygamously married/remarried?

13   What religion do you belong to?

14   What party did you vote for at the last general election?

15   Are you male or female?

16   What job do you do?

17   What is your mother's maiden name?

18   Do you believe women should cover their faces in public?

19   What kind of heating do you have in the place you live in?

20   How much money do you have invested in:

    real estate   Government bonds   stocks and shares   paintings   boats   your own business

21   List your educational qualifications.

22   How many machines with electric motors do you have in your house?

23   How many books by Karl Marx do you own?

24   Have you given or received a dowry?

25   Were you born in this country?

26   Were your parents born in this country?

27   If you lived in South Africa, would you have the vote?

28   What is your annual income?

29   How much tax did you pay last year?

30   What race are you?

3.2 Doctors

BACKGROUND

In many countries the patient does not have an on-going relationship with a general practitioner but will go straight to a specialised doctor. It is therefore worth explaining how the GP system works in the UK, as the questions to be worked on are very much addressed to the family doctor.

IN CLASS

1 Explain to the students how you would go about choosing a new family doctor if you moved to a new area. Ask them what they would do. Suggest that there are many questions you are not socially able to ask a doctor that you might like to ask her/him and that maybe you should be allowed to ask.

2 Give each student a copy of the 'Doctor questions' sheet. Ask them to tick the the questions they feel they would like to be able to ask a new doctor before joining her/his list of patients. Ask them to put a circle by the questions they feel the doctor should be allowed to refuse to answer.

3 Ask them to add any more questions they would like to be allowed to put to a prospective GP.

4 Pair the students and ask them to compare their feelings.

Doctor questions

(Questions you might *want* to ask a doctor before becoming his/her patient. Forget that doctors' high status would make it hard to ask them almost any of the questions below – in this exercise you focus on what *you want* to ask.)

1 Do you smoke?

2 Are you married?

3 How many hours a week do you spend keeping up with new medical information in the journals and on audio cassette?

4 Why did you choose to be a GP rather than a consultant/specialist?

5 How much training in psychiatry did you receive as a student?

6 How good are your relations with the consultants in the local hospital?

7 How good a listener are you?

8 If a case is grave, are you the kind of doctor who is ready to tell the patient the truth?

9 What advice do you give about sterilisation?

10 When a person has mental problems, do you offer them a listening ear or drugs?

11 Who should take medical decisions: the patient after you have informed her/him of the alternatives; you after you have informed the patient of the alternatives; or you without informing the patient of the alternatives?

12 What is your own health record?

13 Under what circumstances would you reveal my medical record to others such as relatives, employers, the police?

14 Which areas did you find most difficult to master in your medical studies?

15 How many children do you have?

16 Do you advise mothers to breast-feed or bottle-feed?

17 Do you give sick notes easily?

18 How much money do you make a year?

19 How much do you talk to your spouse about patients' problems?

20 Why did you decide to become a doctor?

21 How much are you affected by persuasive drug salesmen?

22 Do you think a lot of your work could be done just as well by nurses or less-qualified staff?

23 Do you drink?

24 Have you ever been accused of medical malpractice?

25 How open are you to criticism by patients?

TOPIC	

TOPIC
Matching talents
and interests to
jobs

LANGUAGE
To be involved in
+ gerund; *I'd like
a job* + present
participle (e.g.
*working, looking
after* ...)

LEVEL
Upper
intermediate

TIME
35–50 minutes

MATERIALS
One 'Job'
questionnaire for
each student

3.3 Computer

IN CLASS

1 Ask the students to fill in the questionnaire as if they were seventeen. This part of the exercise can be done prospectively by fifteen year olds and retrospectively by adults. The students work on the questionnaire on their own. Ask the students to put their names on the sheets.

2 Brainstorm a list of fifty to a hundred jobs on the board. The students may want to mention jobs they don't know the word for in English. This is your opportunity to feed the new vocabulary in.

3 Explain that normally the questionnaire would now be fed into a computer which would respond to a student's answers and suggest a list of jobs compatible with that person's requirements. Group the students in threes. Tell the threes they are the computer. Give them three completed questionnaires (not their own) and ask them to come up with suitable jobs for each student's requirements.

4 The 'computers' give the questionnaires back to their owners with a proposed list of jobs.

'Job' questionnaire

	Very important	Quite important	Not sure	Of little or no importance
I'd like a job in which I can use some aspect of:				
1 mathematics	☐	☐	☐	☐
2 physics	☐	☐	☐	☐
3 chemistry	☐	☐	☐	☐
4 biology, botany, or zoology	☐	☐	☐	☐
5 a foreign language	☐	☐	☐	☐
I want to work where there is concern for:				
6 people's health or appearance	☐	☐	☐	☐
7 people's physical safety or security	☐	☐	☐	☐
8 the management of finance	☐	☐	☐	☐
I want to work where I can deal with:				
9 the production of goods	☐	☐	☐	☐
10 the transportation of people, goods, or equipment	☐	☐	☐	☐
11 the sale and distribution of goods	☐	☐	☐	☐
12 the quality of the environment (i.e. the use of land, buildings, and natural resources)	☐	☐	☐	☐
13 the provision of pleasure through goods or services	☐	☐	☐	☐
In my work I'd like to be involved in:				
14 using or appreciating artistic skills	☐	☐	☐	☐
15 making, repairing, or adjusting things	☐	☐	☐	☐
16 finding out how or why things work	☐	☐	☐	☐
17 preparing maps, plans, diagrams, or displays	☐	☐	☐	☐
18 using ideas to write creatively	☐	☐	☐	☐
19 observing behaviour and writing reports	☐	☐	☐	☐
20 checking or calculating figures or data	☐	☐	☐	☐
21 helping or advising people who are in some kind of difficulty	☐	☐	☐	☐
22 persuading people to accept ideas, goods, or services	☐	☐	☐	☐
23 singing, dancing, playing music, acting	☐	☐	☐	☐
24 speaking in public (e.g. at meetings)	☐	☐	☐	☐
I'd like a job:				
25 working outdoors occasionally	☐	☐	☐	☐
26 travelling (locally or abroad)	☐	☐	☐	☐
27 which might lead to self-employment	☐	☐	☐	☐
28 meeting or working with young children	☐	☐	☐	☐
29 which is physically demanding	☐	☐	☐	☐

Now with the help of the questionnaire you have completed, pick out up to nine items which are important to you and place them in order of importance by writing their numbers in the table below.

Most important ☐ ☐ ☐ ☐ ☐ ☐ ☐ ☐ ☐ Least important

<table>
<tr><td>

TOPIC
Female/male
stereotyping

LANGUAGE
Vocabulary:
projective
psychological
testing

LEVEL
Intermediate to
advanced

TIME
30–40 minutes

MATERIALS
One set of
questions for each
pair of students

</td></tr>
</table>

3.4 Woman or man?

BACKGROUND

This questionnaire, taken from the popular Italian weekly, *Oggi*, is unlike most of those in this book. It has a zany, mildly poetical flavour. Some of it is fairly typical of projective psychological questionnaires, in which the person answering is not meant to know how her/his feelings are being measured.

Oggi produced the questionnaire to help people who happen to be born under the sign of Scorpio to discover how 'stinging' they are! In the original magazine presentation, half of the questions were specifically addressed to males and the other half to females.

We have mixed these questions up and used them to get students thinking about male/female stereotypes. It is quite productive, as you read newspapers and magazines, to dream up ways of using questionnaires for new purposes, beyond those their designers had in mind.

IN CLASS

1 If you have a mixed class, form mixed pairs. Tell the students that the male-addressed and female-addressed questions have been mixed up on the sheet you give them. (Explain the background given above.) Tell them their task is to decide which questions were originally addressed to women and which to men, and why. Ten were intended for one sex and ten for the other.

2 Put the numbers of the questions up on the board. Ask one person from each pair to come to the board and to put a ♀ (female) or a ♂ (male) next to each number. General group discussion will tend to focus on particularly contentious questions. Let it flow. Don't intervene and guide.

Note: This is how one colleague wove this exercise into the fabric of their teaching:
'I used it as follow-up work on national/sex stereotyping. Provoked good discussion in pairs, good vocabulary extension. Pairwork took a good twenty minutes so group discussion had to be curtailed. Forty minutes was not long enough for the whole activity. The group discussion revealed many stereotype views which connected closely to the work already done.'

Questionnaire

1 You are the reincarnation of
   a) a martyr
   b) a witch
   c) an artist

2 Your first love is
   a) something you will never forget
   b) the last one too
   c) yet to come

3 Feelings of guilt are
   a) a warning
   b) a form of persecution complex
   c) perfectly normal

4 Your partner is
   a) a liner
   b) a raft
   c) a rubber boat

5 If you come into an inheritance do you
   a) squander it
   b) spend it
   c) save it up

6 You feel yourself to be more important
   a) in an emergency
   b) in humdrum daily life
   c) in unforeseen circumstances

7 You most fear
   a) boredom
   b) extremes
   c) breaking rules

8 Luck is
   a) an illusion
   b) a struggle
   c) fate

9 In love you feel more like
   a) the prey
   b) the hunter
   c) the den

10 You most hate the person who has
   a) betrayed you
   b) hurt you
   c) ignored you

11 You will be reincarnated as
   a) a plant
   b) an animal
   c) a man

12 A person who does not love you
   a) doesn't deserve you
   b) excites you
   c) annihilates you

13 The sea is
   a) a mystery
   b) a stillness
   c) a threat

14 In your choices do you follow
   a) experience
   b) intuition
   c) conscience

15 If a vase smashes to pieces you
   a) buy a new one
   b) try to stick it together again
   c) throw the bits out

16 Choose one of these colours
   a) red
   b) blue
   c) yellow

17 Do you tend to be
   a) too hard
   b) over-tolerant
   c) too much of a liar

18 When you are away on a journey do you, on arrival, immediately ring up
   a) your workplace
   b) your mother
   c) your partner

19 Your strength lies in
   a) your head
   b) your heart
   c) your hands

20 A relationship breaks down in the absence of
   a) understanding
   b) sexual harmony
   c) faithfulness

TOPIC
Patience and
impatience

LANGUAGE
Rich, idiomatic
US English

LEVEL
Intermediate to
advanced

TIME
30–45 minutes

MATERIALS
One 'Behaviour'
questionnaire for
each student

3.5 'A' people and 'B' people

IN CLASS

1. Give out the questionnaires and ask the students to work on them individually.

   If your class is made up of late teenagers, ask them to tick the characteristics that apply to a parent or to a close adult relative. If your class is adult, ask them to tick the characteristics on the 'Behaviour' questionnaire that apply to them.

2 Give the class these numbers:

   4, 8, 17, 20, 22, 24, 27, 28, 31, 32.

   Tell them these are 'B' person characteristics. Ask them to decide what sort of person an 'A' person is. Get them to do this in pairs.

3 Tell the group that according to a ten-year study by Friedman and Rosenman, completed in 1974, 'B' type people between the ages of thirty and sixty are three times less likely than 'A' people to get coronary heart disease. Allow reaction and discussion time.

Acknowledgement: This is an adaptation of an exercise from *Activities for Trainers – 50 Useful Designs*, by Cyril R. Mill (University Associates 1980).

'Behaviour' questionnaire

1   I always move and walk rapidly.

2   I tend to accent key words when I am talking.

3   I eat quickly.

4   I never feel particularly impatient.

5   Sometimes people misunderstand what I say because I speed up my speech at the end of a sentence.

6   If a new gadget comes out or if I see a beautiful piece of bric-à-brac, I like to buy it.

7   I prefer football to baseball because the game moves faster.

8   I schedule my life so that I am hardly ever rushed.

9   A slow driver ahead of me really irritates me.

10   I prefer reading condensations to wading through a whole book.

11   Small talk bores me; I like to talk about things that are important to me.

12   I have equipment in my car for dictating letters and ideas while I drive (or wish I did).

13   I have to read the paper or watch the news while eating a meal.

14   I have a couple of nervous gestures or tics, but they do not bother me much.

15   When I really want to make a point, I am apt to pound on the table.

16   It is hard for me to relax and do nothing. I usually feel guilty if I do not make use of my time.

17   I am never aware of feeling hostile or just plain angry with the world.

18   The prospect of competition makes me raring to go in there and win.

19   Some of the best solutions to problems at work come to me when I am doing something else, such as playing golf or bridge.

20   I work at a steady pace without making any fuss about it.

21   People often point out things around me that I have not noticed, such as a bird or a flower.

22   It does not bother me a bit when I lose in a game, even if I am really pretty good at it.

23   Things often break around me, such as shoelaces, pencil points, and buttons off my clothing, and I grind my teeth.

24   I love to take a vacation and just do nothing.

25   My reports are always in on time or even before they are due; I am efficient in this respect.

26   I enjoy being one up on others, especially the people who are trying so hard to get ahead.

27   I get a lot of relaxation from sports, such as a game of tennis, handball, or swimming.

28   I prefer to talk about other things than successes I have enjoyed.

29   I cannot say no, and my schedule is normally crowded.

30   I have (or would like to have) a long cord on my telephone so that I can walk around while I talk.

31   I can truly say that it does not bother me to be late to a meeting.

32   My philosophy is 'If you miss the plane, there'll be another one soon — no need to sweat.

TOPIC
Areas of
knowledge, their
value and status

LANGUAGE
Vocabulary;
fluency

LEVEL
Post-beginner to
advanced

TIME
40–60 minutes

MATERIALS
One 'Valuing
knowledge' sheet
for each student
Optional selection
of quizzes,
recordings of radio
or TV quiz shows,
examination
syllabuses, etc.

3.6 Valuing knowledge

BACKGROUND
'Knowledge' is a term often used but seldom questioned. In this exercise,
students are invited to consider the knowledge that they and others possess,
and to 'value' it in personal and social frames.

Apart from the necessary (and unpredictable!) vocabulary that the students
will be searching for, the activity is best treated from a language point of view
as a 'free practice' or 'fluency' exercise.

IN CLASS
1 (optional lead-in) Put up the following words on the blackboard:

    HISTORY   SPELLING   CINEMA   ARITHMETIC

Ask the class to think quietly about the uses to which they might put
knowledge of these subjects. Then introduce a few examples of uses, e.g. an
extract from a recording of a radio or TV quiz programme, a newspaper
quiz, an IQ test, an examination paper or list of exam topics, a job
advertisement listing qualifications/expertise, and so on. Allow the students
to talk to their neighbours, or to get up and form loose discussion groups.

2 Give out the 'Valuing knowledge' sheets, one to each student. Ask them to
work on their own to complete the questionnaires. Explain the rating
system, and point out, if necessary, that 'importance' and 'attraction' are
very different ideas, e.g. you might say 'I fully recognise the great importance
of brain surgery in the modern world, but find that kind of work deeply
unattractive.'

3 While the students are working on the questionnaires, remain quietly
available to assist with necessary vocabulary.

4 As the students finish, ask them to group into threes to compare and
discuss their ratings.

'Valuing knowledge' sheet

Rate the following areas of knowledge/skill on a scale of 0–10 according to a) your own knowledge of the subject; b) the importance you give to it; c) how attractive you find it. Write your own suggested topic areas in the spaces provided, and rate them also.

		a) Knowledge	b) Importance	c) Attraction
1	Theatre			
2	....			
3	Translation techniques			
4	....			
5	Football			
6	Military history			
7	Sociology			
8	Mathematics			
9	Care of old people			
10	....			
11	....			
12	Foreign languages – specify:			
13	....			
14	Knitting			
15	Car maintenance			
16	....			
17	Computer science			
18	....			
19	Plumbing			
20	Diet			

When you have finished, find two other people to compare and discuss your answers with.

3.7 Social engineering

BACKGROUND

At a time of innovative fever in science and technology, few people seem to be discussing social inventions, and yet they are all around us. Marriage bureaux had to be invented, as did clubs for the parents of twins. This unit looks at some actual and hypothetical bits of social engineering.

The idea of asking people to discuss advantages, disadvantages and 'intriguing' results is one popularised by Edward de Bono. The third category is an attempt to avoid the polarised thinking of plus and minus.

IN CLASS

1 Draw a picture like this on a board. Explain that a team of aeronautical engineers have designed a plane with the cockpit facing the ground. Ask the students to work in groups of four or five and note down the advantages, disadvantages and intriguing results that would flow from this situation.

2 Before the discussion begins to flag, have a 'messenger' go from group A to group B to report on group A's thinking and so on round the other groups (B sends a messenger to C, C sends a messenger to D, etc.).

Here are some more head situations. Read one to the group:

- The railways have introduced a fare structure by which passengers pay on results. If a journey takes 5% longer than the time stated on the timetable the passenger gets a 5% rebate on her/his fare.

- The telephone company have decided that when a person makes a phone call, the cost of the call is debited to the account of the person on the receiving end.

- The Government has imposed a tax on health. All adults who fail to present their doctor with at least a bona fide 'B' class symptom per year, have to pay a 10% surcharge on their income tax. A wage earner would be exempt providing a spouse presented such a symptom.

- Talk is rationed. Everybody has a 'talk book' stating the number of minutes they can talk each day. At the end of every conversation people must sign each other's 'talk book', stating how long the other talked for.

- The Ministry of Education has decided that too many teachers retain their positions for a lifetime, however bad they are. There are many excellent potential teachers waiting for jobs. The Ministry has decided that one in every ten teachers will be sacked each year. The students in each school are to select the incompetents to be sacked.

- The people in your extended family have decided that on personal feast days (e.g. birthdays) the person whose feast it is has the privilege of giving, rather than receiving presents.
- It has become scientifically possible for a fertilised egg to be implanted in the abdominal wall of a person of either sex. The delivery is by caesarian section.
- A travel group has decided to try mixing two unlikely groups on some of their special package holidays to Spain; the two groups will share villas. On the one hand, teenagers who have recently left home and on the other, parents whose teenage children have recently left home.

These situations already exist:

- Travellers on Japanese 'bullet trains' are given back part of their fare on arrival at destination if the delay has been substantial.
- For seven years people in one of the authors' family have *given* presents on their birthdays.
- Preliminary experiments suggest that men could one day bear children.

TOPIC
The black
economy

LANGUAGE
Vocabulary:
taxation; gerunds

LEVEL
Intermediate to
advanced

TIME
30–40 minutes

MATERIALS
One 'My country'
sheet for every
three students
One 'UK' sheet for
every three
students

3.8 Work and tax

BACKGROUND

Rather than ask people directly what they think or believe about a topic, it can often be more interesting (and even at times more revealing) to ask what they think other people believe. It seems to be a natural human trait to ascribe to others what one holds or feels oneself.

This activity will work very differently in monocultural groups on the one hand, and multicultural groups on the other. In the former case, hard data may well be available to confirm or disprove the students' opinions, as well as to explore the actual structure of taxation and the black economy. In the latter situation, it might perhaps be more useful to concentrate on the underlying similarities and differences between national/cultural attitudes.

IN CLASS

1 Put the students in threes and give to each group one copy of the 'My country' sheet. (If you want students to work together it is better to give just one copy to each group rather than one to each student.)

2 Ask them to work out an estimate of what younger people in their country would feel. If you are working with a multinational or multicultural group, you could ask people of the same background to work together, or else have the students working alone at this stage.

3 Ask each three to write up their estimates on the blackboard or on a sheet of poster paper on the wall. If all the students have the same background this will almost certainly lead to discussion and/or disagreement.

4 Give out the 'UK' sheets to the threesomes. Let them read and discuss the figures together.

5 With groups working in their own country, it would be possible to round off the activity by suggesting that the students actually conduct the survey among friends and acquaintances, in order to check their predictions. This could be done within the school, or in the neighbourhood.

'My country' sheet

We would like to find out what you think younger people in your country feel about earning money 'on the side', i.e. illegally. In your opinion, what percentage of people in your country between the ages of fifteen and twenty-five think these actions are morally wrong?

1   Paying someone in cash so that they don't charge VAT (Sales tax).

2   Accepting cash for work in order to avoid keeping a record for tax purposes.

3   Using an employer's telephone without permission.

4   Paying cash to someone if you suspect he or she isn't paying income tax.

5   Taking time off when you are supposed to be at work.

6   People on the dole earning some money without telling the social security office.

7   Claiming expenses from an employer to which you are not entitled.

8   Taking things home from work without paying for them.

'UK' sheet

The table below was taken from a poll conducted by MORI in Great Britain for *The Times* at the beginning of October 1985 and published in *The Times* on October 28th. The sample used was of 2,058 people over the age of fifteen.

What the people think

We are interested in finding out about public attitudes towards people earning money 'on the side', that is, without declaring it to the tax man. Which of these do you yourself think are morally wrong?

	All ages %	Over-65s	15–25s
Paying someone in cash so that they don't charge VAT	30	44	18
Accepting cash for work in order to avoid keeping a record for tax purposes	35	49	22
Using an employer's telephone without permission	36	53	26
Paying cash to someone if you suspect he/she isn't paying income tax	41	49	28
Taking time off when you're supposed to be at work	66	77	52
People on the dole earning some money without telling the social security office	67	84	51
Claiming expenses from an employer to which you are not entitled	70	79	59
Taking things home from work without paying for them	72	82	63

TOPIC Political manifestos LANGUAGE Vocabulary: political opinion LEVEL Intermediate to advanced TIME 60–90 minutes MATERIALS One 'Values' sheet for each student

3.9 Building parties

BACKGROUND

This exercise is particularly worth doing if you have a fairly mature and politically aware class. There has to be some awareness of importance of the subject in the group for this unit to work. There are also groups in which the unit would be too delicate to handle.

IN CLASS

1 Give out copies of the 'Values' sheet, one to each student. Ask the students, working individually, to go through the sheet marking each statement with a cross in the appropriate column. Answer any *linguistic* questions but avoid giving any personal opinion on the content of the statements. Some of the statements are ambiguous; if students query them, tell them to decide for themselves the interpretation to choose.

2 When the majority of students have finished marking the sheet, ask them to select and mark (e.g. by ringing the appropriate question numbers) the ten statements most important to them individually.

3 All the students should then move around reading each other's completed sheets. The aim is to find someone who has marked at least five of the ten 'important statements' in the same way. When a student finds such a 'kindred spirit', the two of them should continue moving around together to find others who would be prepared to join them in a political party or pressure group.

4 As a further stage (or in a later session), groups should sit together to produce a written 'manifesto'. These would be put up on the walls for others to read, or copied and circulated among the whole class.

Acknowledgement: The idea of using questionnaires to form groups came to us from Richard Baudains. The use of 'value clarification' questionnaires in general has its origin in the US. Valuable sources for the use and construction of these can be found in: *Values Clarification*, by Simon, Howe and Kirschenbaum, New York, Hart 1972.

'Values' sheet

		Strongly agree	Neutral or uncertain	Strongly disagree
1	People are essentially good.			
2	Power corrupts.			
3	Everyone has a right to free medical attention when ill.			
4	It is more important for the law to protect the innocent than to punish the guilty.			
5	The death penalty is essential for murder and other serious crimes.			
6	It is better to tax spending than to tax earning.			
7	Property is theft.			
8	Market forces are a better regulator of the economy than government control.			
9	People who cannot find work should turn to their family and friends for help, not to the government.			
10	There's no changing human nature.			
11	The use of weapons can never be justified.			
12	Private education creates divisions in society, and should be forbidden by law.			
13	Some jobs should never be done by women.			
14	The basis of any social system should be a body of religious belief.			
15	Books, newspapers, films and TV should be free of all censorship on moral grounds.			
16	The group is more important than the the individual.			
17	My highest duty is to my country.			
18	There should be a minimum wage.			
19	There should be a maximum wage.			
20	Unearned income should be taxed more heavily than earned income.			
21	Marriage should be a matter for agreement between the two people involved; it is not the responsibility of the state or any other outside body.			
22	Democracy is an illusion.			
23	Parents should be held responsible for their children's actions until the children are at least 14 years of age.			
24	Up to 18, one must have the permission of one's parents before one can leave home, enter employment, or get married.			
25	Everyone should have the right to vote at the age of 16.			
26	Passports should be abolished.			
27	The important industries of a state should be controlled by the government.			
28	Much more public money should be spent on providing theatres, concert halls and art galleries for the people.			
29	Religion should be taught compulsorily in schools			

3.10 Lies

BACKGROUND

Telling lies can be an effective way of clarifying the truth. In the first part of this activity, students are asked to guess whether questions have been answered truthfully or falsely. In discussion afterwards, the truth emerges more powerfully. In the second stage, students are asked to talk about themselves totally untruthfully; here the truth is revealed by implication.

The language of the exercise is kept deliberately simple, and the topic parallels the contents of many coursebooks. It should be quite within the language capacity of even elementary students.

IN CLASS

1 Pair the students.

2 Give one student in each pair a question sheet and the other a five-item list. Neither should show their sheet to the other.

3 Explain the rules of the game carefully:
   – The questioners should ask the questions on their sheets one by one, saying the number of each question loudly and clearly.
   – The answerer checks his/her number list. If the number of the question appears on the number list she/he must give a *false* answer. If the number does *not* occur on the list the answerer must give a true reply.
   – After each answer the questioner should silently put down whether the answer *seemed* to him/her true or false.

4 When all the questions have been asked and answered the questioner tries to identify which answers were false. The answerer confirms or denies.

5 Tell the pairs to do the exercise the other way round – this time the person who questioned before has to answer the questions. Give the new answerers *different* number lists. The students work through steps one to four as outlined above.

6 Bring pairs of students together in fours or sixes. Ask them to answer these questions:
   – How many of the five false answers did you get?
   – What clues did the answerer offer you?
   – How difficult did you find it to lie when you were answering?
   – Do you normally know when someone is lying – what gives them away?
   – When were you last lied to, by whom and about what?

7 Ask the students to form new pairs. Tell them that each must talk to the other about him/herself for three to five minutes, but that everything they say must be a lie.

Note: If you find this activity productive you might like to look at 'Fibs and Bloody Great Lies', in Philip Ely's book *Bring the Lab Back to Life*, (Prentice Hall 1984).

Question sheet

1 How many doors are there in your home?

2 What kitchen smells do you really dislike?

3 Do you like having animals in the house?

4 What are the first sounds you normally hear in the morning?

5 If you opened your fridge door now, what would you see?

6 Where is the biggest window in your house?

7 How many chairs are there in your home?

8 Where do you have the telephone in your home?

9 What sounds in your house most annoy you?

10 How long have you lived in your present place?

11 Are you happy with the place you have your cooker?

12 What additional piece of furniture would you like in your home?

13 What repairs to your home still need to be done?

14 How long do you expect to go on living in your present place?

15 How many doors are there in your house?

Number lists (to be cut up)

1	7	6	5	2
3	8	9	9	3
5	9	11	1	6
7	12	13	15	10
14	14	15	4	13

4	2	1	3	2
8	4	4	6	7
12	8	7	10	11
13	12	10	14	12
15	14	13	15	14

TOPIC
The morality of
advertising

LANGUAGE
Vocabulary:
journalistic

LEVEL
Intermediate to
advanced

TIME
30–45 minutes

MATERIALS
One 'Advertising'
questionnaire for
every three
students

3.11 Advertising limits

BACKGROUND

This exercise is about the morality of advertising, but it is also about how well your students know each other. The heart of the exercise is hypothesising how someone else in the group would answer the questionnaire. Each learner is thinking about the topic, but simultaneously about how another person may react to it.

IN CLASS

1 Put the students in threes and give person A the questionnaire. A asks B and C the questions.

2 'Twin' the threesomes, for example by giving each threesome a coloured card so that there are two red groups, two blue groups, etc. Try to arrange the class so that twinned groups are sitting far apart from one another. Each group is to choose one member of its twin group to think about. They then go through the questionnaire again, this time deciding how they think that person would have answered each question.

3 The threesomes come together in groups of six and check if what they thought was right.

'Advertising' questionnaire

1 In a medical advertisement is it acceptable to claim that your product cures a given illness? Why/Why not?

2 Is it permissible to advertise breath-testing devices to be used by drivers? Why/Why not?

3 Is it acceptable for alcoholic drink ads to link social, business and sexual success with drinking? Why/Why not?

4 How old should people shown in cigarette adverts be? Why?

5 Is it acceptable to compare your product to its rivals on the market in such a way as to show that they are inferior? Why/Why not?

6 Should you be allowed to advertise correspondence courses in Judo, Karate and other martial arts? Why/Why not?

7 Should you be allowed to advertise jemmies and bugging devices? Why/Why not?

8 Can a medical advertisement promise to refund money to dissatisfied customers? Why/Why not?

9 Should a political party run TV adverts on polling day? Why/Why not?

10 Is it acceptable to play on people's fear and guilt when advertising a product? Why/Why not?

11 Which services/products do you feel it should be illegal to advertise and why?

12 Is the flashing of subliminal images in TV advertising acceptable?

13 What techniques would you like to see banned from TV, hoarding and magazine advertising?

Section 4
Free oral practice

It's a cliche that spontaneity needs to be worked at. For students to ask and answer questions freely, it may be necessary to help them, through games or other exercises, to get used, for example, to:

– listening to what other students say; many students are accustomed (or have been trained) to value only the words of the teacher or the coursebook or the cassette recorder

– being the centre of class attention, e.g. by answering questions from the front of the class

– being prepared to express and enjoy their own imaginations, and to value imaginative as well as 'factual' expression

– accepting and profiting from situations where the teacher is not overtly in control, as in many small-group activities

The 'doubling' technique used in 4.2 to 4.5 is a form of role-play in which one person gives voice to the thoughts, feelings, etc. of another (present or absent). It differs from conventional role-play in that the 'double' is asked to speak for a real, individual person rather than merely construct an ideal or stereotype.

For the speaker, doubling is an effective way of going beyond one's own narrow point of view on a person or situation; speaking *as* rather than *about* a third person sharpens perceptions and increases empathy. For the listener, the double acts as a clear, concrete focus of attention.

TOPIC
Various

LANGUAGE
Oral
confidence-
building; mixed
questions

LEVEL
Elementary to
advanced

TIME
15–20 minutes
(for each game)

MATERIALS
None

4.1 Question games

BACKGROUND

We have found the following games useful in helping students to ask and answer questions freely, especially where they have not been used, for example, to listening to what other students say or being the centre of class attention. Many of the familiar party and language-teaching games can also be used or adapted to achieve these aims, as well as giving useful practice in the language forms (e.g. Alibi; Animal, Vegetable & Mineral; What's My Line?). Suggestions for good books on games can be found in the Bibliography on page 00.

A. Guessing games

To reverse the all-too-frequent pattern in which the teacher asks the questions and the student answers:

Before the class begins, draw (on a hidden blackboard or a large piece of paper) a very simple picture (e.g. two or three people in various attitudes, the furniture in a room, a map, an abstract made of clear simple geometrical shapes). The students must then ask questions to find out exactly what the picture shows.

Similar games include: guessing the contents of a bag; building a model (in Lego or with a kit); finding out a story by asking questions.

B. Lies

In traditional games such as 'Alibi' and 'Spot-the-Lie', people are asked to discover which of a person's answers are true and which false. A more imaginative and creative activity is for one person to answer questions from a group (or partner in pairwork) giving *only* untruthful answers.

The game can be played as a purely imaginative exercise, or it can be made competitive by attempting to catch the liar out in factual or logical inconsistencies.

C. Press conference

To check the group's comprehension of a reading or listening text, teachers often ask students oral or written 'comprehension questions'. Where the text is concerned with *people* (e.g. newspaper article, short story, coursebook dialogue, recorded conversation or playlet) the same can be achieved, with more energy and enjoyment, through question-and-answer role-play:

For each character in the text, one student sits in front of the class to answer questions in the role of that character. The rest of the students are journalists interviewing them at a press conference. At first, let the journalists concentrate on 'factual' questions, i.e. ones that can be answered definitely according to information in the text. Then encourage them to ask questions which cannot be answered in this way, but which lead the interviewees to use their imagination to develop the characters they are representing.

This activity can also be done with pictures. Put up, or ask students to choose, one or more large magazine pictures of people. These should be definite and characterful. One member of the group stands or sits by each picture and answers questions addressed to the person in their picture (e.g. as an interpreter). (The 'interpreters' may also want to ask each other questions.) The activity works well if the pictures are strongly contrasted.

4.2 The driving instructor

TOPIC
The driving test;
adulthood

LANGUAGE
Fluency; mixed
questions

LEVEL
Elementary to
advanced

TIME
25–45 minutes
(stages 1–5)

MATERIALS
None

BACKGROUND

This activity is designed principally for people in the age range fifteen to twenty, when the driving test is particularly important as a 'rite of passage' in many cultures; thoughts and questions about driving tests and instructors are often also about being or becoming an adult.

IN CLASS

1 Have a student at the board to act as secretary. Ask the class to shout out all the words that come to their minds when you give them the key phrase: DRIVING TEST. The secretary writes them up all over the blackboard.

2 Ask people who have taken the driving test to say a few words about what it was like for them.

3 Each student now writes ten to fifteen questions addressed to a driving instructor about her/his feelings, thoughts, knowledge, etc., e.g. 'Why is there no training on motorways?' 'Have you often felt frightened?'

4 Ask one of the people who is preparing for or has fairly recently taken a driving test to describe their instructor and their feelings towards her/him. After a while, ask this student to 'double' (see 'Oral work', p. 81) for the instructor, sitting in a chair the way this driving instructor would sit. Get other students to ask her/him questions; the 'driving instructor' answers in role.

5 Have the students sit in groups of four to six to repeat stage 4. They can use the questions they have prepared, or ask spontaneously, as they choose.

6 If the mood of the class is right, and if there is sufficient time, allow a discussion to develop on the status of the driving test in people's lives.

TOPIC
People I know

LANGUAGE
Fluency; mixed questions; language of describing people

LEVEL
Post-beginner to intermediate

TIME
20–40 minutes

MATERIALS
None

4.3 The empty chair

BACKGROUND

In this, the simplest of 'doubling' exercises, students are invited to think about and introduce to the rest of the class people they know well. At the least, the activity motivates otherwise uninspired drilling in question forms; at best, it deepens the relations of group members to each other and invests the language class with important features of the real world.

Asking students to write their questions down before putting them orally ensures that a) there is ample thinking time and b) the student has the opportunity to get language help from the teacher or a fellow-student. With some groups, this stage may not be necessary. In any case, there should be no insistence that *all* or *only* the written questions may be put.

IN CLASS

1 Place an empty chair in front of the group, and invite one of the students to fill it by describing someone he/she knows well. (This should *not* be someone physically present in the group.) The description should enable the others to have a picture of the person's appearance and character.

2 Everyone writes ten questions addressed to the person in the empty chair. If practice on specific question forms is wanted (e.g. *Where* ...? or ... *did* ...? questions), this can be built in at this stage.

3 The student who 'filled' the chair now goes and actually sits in it, and answers the group's questions *in the role* of the person previously described. We remember one class in which an eighteen-year-old Catalan girl impersonated her father on the chair. She had described him as owning and running a restaurant and many of the questions fired at her were about his work. The amazing thing was that she seemed to look more and more middle-aged and male as the interview progressed! Somehow the group managed to confirm her in that role, which she clearly enjoyed being in.

4 Repeat the activity, either with a new student filling the chair for the whole class, or else in smaller groups (four to eight) with the members each taking turns to fill the chair.

Note: As well as its uses in the class, this exercise can be used in one-to-one teaching to expand the number of people 'present' in the session. If both student and teacher act as doubles, quite complex and rewarding role-plays can be developed.

<table>
<tr><td>

TOPIC
Self and others

LANGUAGE
Fluency; mixed
questions;
reported speech

LEVEL
Post-beginner to
intermediate

TIME
20–30 minutes

MATERIALS
None

</td></tr>
</table>

4.4 Proxy answers

BACKGROUND

This exercise centres on the knowledge that some people in a classroom have of one another, and is best attempted after the students have worked together for a while. The opening 'modelling' by the teacher should be kept as short as possible; the aim is not to focus on the teacher but on the students.

IN CLASS

1 Ask the class to think of questions that they might like to ask you about yourself. If you like, suggest one or two areas that might be worth exploring. Don't let them ask the questions yet.

2 Sit in front of the class where everyone can see you, and invite two or three students to come out and sit with you. Ask the rest of the class to start putting their questions to you, but explain that you are not going to answer their questions yourself. Instead the people with you answer in your place, using the first person 'I'.

3 After four or five questions have been asked and answered, stop the questioning. You may, if you wish, comment on the answers that have been given for you. Your comments are listened to with great attention by the people who have answered for you, especially if they got things factually wrong, as frequently happens.

4 Find a volunteer in the group who is prepared to act in the same way. He/she comes and sits in front of the group. The rest of the class write questions to her/him on slips of paper, and he/she also writes questions to herself/himself. (There is an opportunity here for the teacher to assist the weaker students in composing their questions.)

5. The volunteer now selects two or three fellow students to sit with her/him. Collect up the question slips (including those written by the volunteer herself/himself) and redistribute them among the group. The activity then continues as in stages 1 and 2 above.

6 Once the questioning has run its course, ask the volunteer to correct or expand any answers given for her/him. (This can also turn into useful practice in reported speech.)

Note: An example of the classroom use of this activity can be found on the teacher-training video 'See for Yourself' (details in Bibliography, page 142). The volunteer on the video was asked a wide selection of questions including:

– Did you have an idol as a child?
– Would you like to live in London for the rest of your life?
– Did you have nightmares as a child?
– Do you approve of mercy-killing?

TOPIC
The natural world

LANGUAGE
Fluency; mixed
questions

LEVEL
Elementary to
intermediate (if
you use the letter
text)
or
Intermediate to
advanced (if you
use the scientific
text)

TIME
20–30 minutes

MATERIALS
An earthworm in a
pot of damp soil
(you will easily
find a worm by
digging over a
small piece of
garden)
One copy of 'The
Earthworm' and/or
'Letter from a
Worm' for each
student

4.5 The worm

BACKGROUND
Here, the doubling technique of the previous activities is applied to non-human subjects. We have successfully used it with possessions (a person's shoes, spectacles, notebook, etc.), furniture, indoor plants, and the classroom itself. If the students and the teacher are willing to enter the (academically odd) frame of the exercise, the direct questioning can be far more powerful than just 'talking about' the theme.

The texts that follow the questioning stage of the activity are included in response to requests by classes for more information about the subject.

As with the previous exercises in this section, there should be no insistence that *all* or *only* the written questions may be put.

IN CLASS
1 Put the worm where the class can see it clearly. Tell the students that they are going to interview the worm.

2 Ask the students to write down eight to ten questions they would like to ask the worm. Make sure they write direct, second person questions, e.g. 'Worm, do you like the rain?'

3 Tell the class that the worm would be happy to answer their questions, but has lost its voice. Invite one member of the class to come and speak for the worm. The rest of the class then put their questions to the worm, and the 'double' answers.

4 There are usually plenty of questions about the worm's life that no one in the group has an answer to. If this is so, give out one or other of the texts ('Letter from a Worm', and 'The Earthworm') or supply your own text.

VARIATION
As the students are writing their questions find a person to speak for the worm and supply him/her with one or other of the texts. She/he then has the information to answer some of the questions that will be asked. The only snag with this variation is that the rest of the students will come on to the reading assignment with less thirst for knowledge than in the sequence outlined above, since the student speaking for the worm will have already given them most of the information.

Letter from a worm

Dear Student,

You are very odd with your eyes and ears. I don't have any of these but I have a sense of touch all over my body. I *feel* chemicals and light all over me and react to these.

I burrow through the earth and a lot of it passes through my body. I break the earth up and the gardeners like me because this improves the soil. I drag leaves down into my burrow, too.

You may wonder which sex I am. I'm both male and female. I produce young worms by coming up to the surface of the soil at night and lying against another worm. We exchange sperm. I give sperm from my male organ and receive it in my female one. I then produce eggs in a cocoon. The young worms come out of the cocoon.

My heart is not at all like yours. It's in rings round my stomach in the front half of my body.

The thing I really hate is great heat. I must stay moist. If it gets too hot or too cold, I burrow deep down into the soil. I cover myself with mucus that hardens and keeps me moist. I can stay quiet like this for a very long time.

I quite like rain, but not too much. If it rains too hard, my burrow gets flooded and I might drown. I hate thrushes, moles and hedgehogs.

Yours sincerely,

The earthworm

The Earthworm

Earthworms live in loose or compact soil. They come to the surface at night or after the burrow has been flooded by heavy rain.

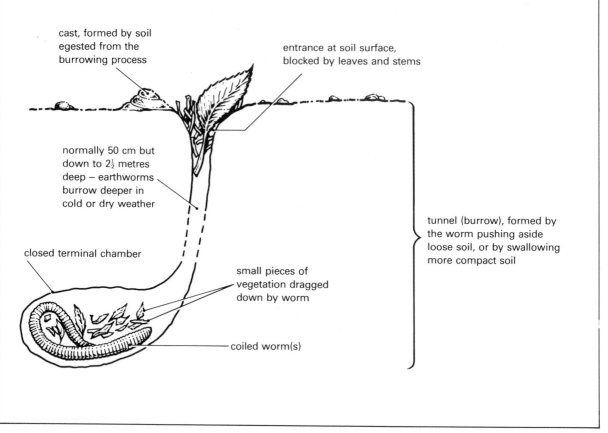

cast, formed by soil egested from the burrowing process

entrance at soil surface, blocked by leaves and stems

normally 50 cm but down to 2½ metres deep — earthworms burrow deeper in cold or dry weather

tunnel (burrow), formed by the worm pushing aside loose soil, or by swallowing more compact soil

closed terminal chamber

small pieces of vegetation dragged down by worm

coiled worm(s)

Earthworms are found in all but the most acid soils. In soils rich in humus as many as two million worms per acre may be present.

The importance of earthworms in maintaining soil fertility was noted as long ago as 1777 by the naturalist the Rev. Gilbert White. Excellent experiments on this aspect of the earthworm's activities were carried out around 1880 by Charles Darwin, who kept worms in pots containing garden soil and described the ways with which they dealt with various types of vegetation given to them. Darwin also collected worm casts from measured areas of land and estimated that about ten tons per acre were produced annually, equivalent to a complete covering of 4 mm, though this is probably an over-estimate. Darwin spread chalk lumps and cinders on the soil surface and found that in less than thirty years the activity of earthworms had buried them 20 cm deep.

Summary of the **beneficial** effects of earthworms in soil:

1 Their burrows
   (i) provide natural drainage channels
   (ii) bring air down into the soil .
   (iii) allow the thicker roots of plants to penetrate more easily.

2 As worms ingest only fine (clay and silt) particles, these are selectively deposited at the surface – sand is left below. The fine particles provide a good tilth (seed bed).

3 The action of the worm's gizzard in breaking up the soil and egesting it as fine casts also provides a good tilth.

4 The worm ingests soil at a lower level and egests casts at the surface – this mixes soil from lower layers with those at the surface and increases the depth of topsoil.

5 By dragging organic remains into their burrows, these remains become mixed with soil more quickly – they are decomposed more quickly by soil bacteria to form future plant food.

6 Urine and faeces from the worm add manure to the soil and encourage the activity of soil bacteria.

7 The worm's oesophagus glands neutralise slightly acid soils when these soils are ingested.

The activities of worms are **detrimental** to lawns – the excavations spoil the lawn surface, cause bare patches and encourage the growth of moss.

TOPIC
Childhood

LANGUAGE
Fluency;
present tenses

LEVEL
Lower
intermediate to
advanced

TIME
25–45 minutes

MATERIALS
None

4.6 Time travel interview

BACKGROUND

Particularly for adults, the evocation of childhood is a compelling topic; even the shyest, linguistically least forthcoming student can often be drawn out by the choice of suitable childhood themes.

One should only introduce this activity if the group members know each other and get along together reasonably well, and after one or more warm-up activities. Precisely what sort of warm-up to use is a matter for the teacher to decide; we propose two that we have found of wide application.

IN CLASS

Warm-up A: Ask the class to sit comfortably and relaxed, preferably in a circle or in small groups. If possible, dim the lights or pull down some of the blinds. Then, in a clear but quiet voice, lead the group through a short guided fantasy on the theme of childhood, e.g. by saying the following, allowing fifteen to twenty seconds pause between each phrase: 'It's warm ... You can feel the sun on your face ... You are very young, five or six years old ... Your feet are bare, you can feel the ground ... Start walking, slowly ... Feel the ground under your feet ...' After a few minutes' silence, invite the students to share their impressions, memories, images, with someone sitting near them.

Warm-up B: Ask the students to get up and walk around the room (or in the corridor or outside the school building). Tell them that as they walk, they should think of a place where they walked as a child, and to imagine the route and the places along it. When ready, each student should invite another to accompany him/her on the walk, and tell their partner something of what it is/was like.

1 (optional) Model the activity yourself briefly, in front of the whole class. Imagine yourself at the age of five or six or seven. Tell the class what you are wearing and where you live. Invite them to ask you questions about yourself at that age. (It is impossible to say what your group may ask you. We have been asked opening questions like:
   – What did you have for breakfast today?
   – Who takes you to school?
   – Who's your special friend? etc.)
   Answer in role, i.e. in the present tense and from the point of view of the person you then were. Answer just three or four questions before passing the exercise back to them. *Or*, better, before class, explain the exercise to a student you feel would do the activity comfortably and well. Then, in class, ask her/him to model it as above.

2 Ask the class to form groups of four to seven members. If possible, have each group sitting in a small circle, so that all can see and hear one another easily. One member in each group should then start to answer questions from the others in the role of herself/himself at a younger age. Many people find it helpful in such role-plays to imagine and take on physical aspects of the role first, e.g. body posture and gestures.

3 When one interviewee in a group has finished, another may take her/his place. Alternatively, the group might prefer to discuss what has happened, or the memories of childhood that were awakened in the questioners.

4 It is superfluous to try to 'round off' the activity with a general discussion or other follow-up exercise; let the session end in the quiet, intimate mood produced by stage 3 above.

TOPIC
Hobbies and
professions

LANGUAGE
Fluency; mixed
questions

LEVEL
Post-beginner to
advanced

TIME
15–20 minutes
(for each round)

MATERIALS
None

4.7 Which one?

BEFORE CLASS

Interview privately three people from a class that knows more English than the one you are teaching. One of the three should have an unusual hobby or sport. Let the other two question her/him so they get to have a pretty good idea about the person and their unusual hobby.

IN CLASS

1 The three more advanced students come into your class and they introduce themselves as all having the same unusual hobby. Tell the class that only one of them is telling the truth – the other two are fakers.

2 Your class now has two minutes in which to question each of them and try to find which one is telling the truth. The questions must be about the hobby: 'Are you telling the truth?' would not be in order; 'When did you first start (potholing etc.)?' would be acceptable.

3 After the questioning, let the class discuss the evidence they have, either all together or in small groups.

4 Finally, the class (or all the members of small groups) vote on who is the real hobbyist. Further questions about the hobby could be asked after this.

VARIATIONS

The game can be played time and again – in fact it improves with playing. Areas for questioning can include:

an unusual profession
a parent's profession
an unusual place where one lived
an odd dream
an unusual journey
an unexpected meal
an important success

(There need to be many more cross-class activities in which older learners interact with younger ones, and higher-level learners show off their knowledge in ways that are genuinely useful to lower-level classes. This exercise offers one of many possible frames.)

Acknowledgement: The activity derives from the Channel 4 TV game 'Tell the Truth'. A similar game, using pictures, is described by Randal Holme in *Recipes for Tired Teachers*, ed. Christopher Sion (Addison Wesley, 1985).

Section 5

Personalised dictations

Dictation has virtues:

- In learning a language such as English, where the correspondence between a spoken sentence and its written representation is complex, dictation is a technically useful exercise
- It is safe for a linguistically diffident teacher to use
- It can have a calming effect on a group's mood
- It can provide mental preparation time for a communicative exercise

This last aspect is the one explored in this section. In the dictations we propose, the students are invited to take down the text while simultaneously thinking about their reactions to it. They note down their reaction to each sentence after it has been dictated. The students are involved in double processing; linguistic decoding and encoding as well as noting their reaction to the meaning. The brain is working on two cylinders instead of one.

The thinking/deciding/reaction process during the dictation flows naturally into exchanging impressions with a neighbour immediately after. Correcting language errors in the writing is a possible third stage.

More exercises on this model are to be found in *Dictation*, Davis et al (CUP 1988).

TOPIC
Personal
mnemonic devices

LANGUAGE
Present simple
tense

LEVEL
Elementary to
intermediate

TIME
40–55 minutes

MATERIALS
One 'Memory'
dictation grid for
each student
One 'Memory'
dictation for each
student

5.1 Your memory

BACKGROUND
(see 1.8).

IN CLASS

1 Pre-teach any of the words in the 'Memory' dictation that you feel the students may not know.

2 Explain that you will dictate the questionnaire and that after each sentence they are to answer the question personally by ticking the correct frequency column.

3 Dictate the questions, leaving time for thought and ticking.

4 Pair the students with different people and get them to correct each other's dictation. When they are halfway through the process, give them copies of the dictation for them to check against.

5 Students may be interested to check on how they actually do go about memorising and recalling. Tell them you're going to try a small experiment with them:

a) Show them a picture of a person and firmly name the person, using first name, initial and family name. The person should not be previously known to the group. Remove the picture from sight. No one must write.

b) Clearly but quickly tell them your home phone number. No one must write.

c) Ask the group how many days there are in October.

d) Ask someone to describe a road he/she has driven or been driven along once.

e) Ask everybody to write down your home phone number.

f) Show the picture to the group, and ask everybody to write down the name, initial and family name of the person.

6 Allow a general discussion to ensue on the techniques used.

Acknowledgement: This questionnaire derives from one in *Your Memory* by Alan Baddely (Penguin 1982).

'Memory' dictation

1   Do you use an alarm clock?

2   Do you write out shopping lists?

3   Do you keep a diary for future events?

4   Do you write things you have to remember on your hand/arm/leg?

5   Do you write yourself 'things to do' lists?

6   Do you ask other people to remind you of things?

7   Do you use rhymes to remember things?

8   When you cook, do you use the oven-timer?

9   Do you write things on the calendar on the wall?

10   When you lose something, do you reconstruct what you did with it in your head?

11   When you hear a new phone number, do you remember it straight off?

12   Do you put things in odd places to remember them?

13   When you lose something, do you panic?

14   When you hear a new phone number, do you repeat it to yourself to remember it?

15   Do you use your knuckles to remember the length of the months?

16   If you have driven along a road once, do you remember it clearly?

17   Can you remember a person's name two minutes after you have been introduced to them?

'Memory' dictation grid

	never	seldom	sometimes	often	always
1					
2					
3					
4					
5					
6					
7					
8					
9					
10					
11					
12					
13					
14					
15					
16					
17					

TOPIC
The heroic vision
of oneself

LANGUAGE
Must and *should*

LEVEL
Intermediate to
advanced

TIME
25–40 minutes

MATERIALS
The statements
below on an
overhead
transparency

5.2 Too good to be true

BACKGROUND

Many people make themselves unhappy by striving to achieve an impossible/
undesirable vision of self. The statements below are mostly unhelpful to sensible
living, but some are more so than others. It depends on the person.

IN CLASS

1 Ask each student to tear a sheet of paper into eleven strips. Tell the students
you are going to dictate some statements to them – they should take each
statement down on a different slip of paper. In the course of the dictation
they are to place the statements in rank order on the desk in front of them.
Give them time during the dictation to change the order of their bits of paper.

2 Do *not* read all the statements to them first. Go straight in and dictate the first
statement. As you go through, allow time for thinking and changing the order.

3 When the dictation is over, ask the students to compare their rankings with
their neighbours.

4 Ask them to correct their spelling, etc. with the help of your overhead
transparency of the statements.

5 Put the students in fours to come up with more 'too good to be true' statements.
(You might want to use some of these in future runs of the exercise).

Acknowledgement: This exercise derives from A. Ellis, (1958) 'Rational
Psychotherapy' in *Journal of General Psychotherapy* 59, pp 35–49.

Statement sheet

- It is necessary for an adult to be loved and approved of by everybody.
- To be considered worthwhile one must be competent, adequate and achieving in every
  possible way.
- External events, beyond our personal responsibility and control, frustrate and make us
  unhappy.
- We have no way of changing our life circumstances to make them fit better with our need.
- Men shouldn't cry.
- It is a catastrophe when things don't go the way we want them to.
- To express anger is to lose control and is wrong.
- If I love someone, that person should be happy and appreciative.
- Being emotional is a sign of weakness.
- If I haven't lived up to my expectations, I must be a failure.
- If I am not happy it is because the other person does not really love me.

TOPIC
The groups you
have belonged to
in your life

LANGUAGE
Present simple
tense

LEVEL
Post-beginner to
advanced

TIME
30–40 minutes

MATERIALS
One 'First person
plural' dictation
sheet for each
student
One set of
questions for each
student

5.3 First person plural

BACKGROUND

In this exercise, students are asked questions that naturally provoke an individual 'me on my own' response – they are asked to answer in terms of self *and* one or more others. The power of the exercise derives from the shock of remembering how the 'I' belongs and has belonged to various 'we's.

Take question 2: *Which year were you born in?*
If you happened to have a twin you might well write 'We were born in 19...' thinking of your twin as the other half of the 'we'. You might write the same formal sentence and be thinking of two or three of your school friends who were born in the same year as you. You might take a much broader view, as Salmon Rushdie did in *Midnight's Children*, and think of all the people in your country born on that day.

The exercise is a delicate one. Do not use it until people in the group know each other reasonably well.

IN CLASS

1 Pre-teach any unknown words in the dictation questions.

2 Explain that you will dictate the questionnaire sentence by sentence. After each question you will leave time for the students to write their answers. The only rule is that they must include 'we' in their answers instead of 'I', and must think of the group they belong to or belonged to that the 'we' represents.

3 Dictate the questions, leaving time for them to write their answers.

4 Pair the students and ask them to explain their answers to a partner. This will entail telling the partner who the people in the 'we' are.

5 Ask the students to correct their dictations and answers. Go round helping. Then give out the set of questions.

'First person plural' questionnaire

1   What sort of music do you like?

2   Which year were you born in?

3   What languages do you speak?

4   How much TV do you watch?

5   What games did you play when you were nine?

6   What subjects were you good at when you were thirteen?

7   Did you like your primary school?

8   Are you good at swimming?

9   Which is your favourite place to shop?

10   Where did you go on holiday last year?

11   How often do you go to church?

12   Have you been ill in your life?

13   How much alcohol do you drink a week?

14   Whom do you most admire?

'First person plural' dictation sheet

1 _____

We _____

2 _____

We _____

3 _____

We _____

4 _____

We _____

5 _____

We _____

6 _____

We _____

7 _____

We _____

8 _____

We _____

9 _____

We _____

10 _____

We _____

11 _____

We _____

12 _____

We _____

13 _____

We _____

14 _____

We _____

5.4 Ordinary criminality

TOPIC
Personal morality

LANGUAGE
Have you ever +
past participle
(UK), contrasted
with *Did you
ever* + infinitive
(US)

LEVEL
Upper
intermediate

TIME
40–55 minutes

MATERIALS
One 'Criminal
dictation' grid for
each student
One 'Criminal
dictation' for each
student

BACKGROUND

The students are asked to guess/estimate the percentage of people in their country who have committed a given crime. It is irrelevant how accurate they are. The point of the guesstimate is what it says about the student and her/his vision of her/his country.

After the exercise you may want to go into the social and legal differences between the UK and the students' country/countries.

This exercise can be used by itself as a means of bringing attention and interest to dictation, or as a warm-up to further work (e.g. reading comprehension, essay writing) on the theme of crime in society.

IN CLASS

1 Give out one copy of the 'Criminal dictation' grid to each student. Tell the class you are going to dictate a list of fifteen criminal actions for them to write in the left-hand column of the grid. After each item has been dictated, they should estimate the percentage of people in their country who have probably committed the crime.

2 Dictate the 'Criminal dictation' given.

3 Ask the students to get into groups of three to five to look at each other's guesstimates and discuss them. Also ask them to decide on a suitable maximum punishment for each action.

4 Give out the 'Criminal dictation' sheets to each student for language checking.

Acknowledgement: Open University Foundation Course in Sociology.

Language Note: In this exercise we expose students to a mixture of US and UK grammatical usage. This is why we suggest the exercise should only be used at *upper* intermediate level. At lower levels it might well confuse. The mixing of the two varieties is very common in TV situations and many intermediate and above students are interested in the differences.

Criminal dictation

1 Have you ever taken out more money than you had in your bank account?

2 Have you ever avoided paying your TV licence fee?

3 Have you ever travelled on the underground without paying the fare?

4 Have you ever broken the speed limit?

5 Did you ever bribe a garage to pass your car as fit to drive?

6 Have you ever evaded customs duty?

7 Did you ever steal stationery from your place of work?

8 Have you ever used your company telephone to make personal telephone calls?

9 When given too much change by a shopkeeper, have you ever kept it?

10 Have you ever travelled first class on a second class ticket?

11 Did you ever wind back the speedometer on your car?

12 Have you ever kept money that you found?

13 Have you ever cheated on expenses?

14 Have you ever taken 'souvenirs' from a hotel?

15 Have you ever lied about your income to the tax authorities?

Criminal dictation grid

% of people in my country who have probably committed these crimes in these two age groups:

	10–25	50–60
1		
2		
3		
4		
5		
6		
7		
8		
9		
10		
11		
12		
13		
14		
15		

WRITING

Students write questionnaires

The Writer's Rights

Writing done only for one's own eyes answers a deeply felt need; journals, notes to oneself, jotted thoughts, diaries, are some of the results. All other writing presumes an addressee, a reader interested in some way in the content of the writing. If you, gentle colleague, don't read this sentence, why should I want to start writing it?

In class, students often write essays or stories or exercises intended only for the eye of the teacher, an eye that is sometimes more drawn towards form than human content. Their writings are marked, numbered, percentaged and then given back for the students to . . . – what? Beat their breasts when their interlanguage is different from their teacher's view of how the language should be? Recall the thoughts they had while deciding what to write? Think about new things to write? Feel relieved because there is less green or red on this script than on other recent homework?

Why should the student be treated so differently from other writers and alone denied the basic right to an interested reader? After all, there are plenty of candidates for this role:

- Someone outside the group, for example, penpals abroad. There are children in Naples who have correspondence in English with children in Salonica.
- The teacher, as a fellow human being. Some teachers find a personal letter exchange with their students to be very fruitful, both linguistically and personally. (See ELTJ, Vol 37/1, Jan 1983.)
- Each other. In their writing classes in ESIEE, Paris, Kris Markowski and Michael Gradwell encourage each student to write short signed letters to others in the group. Those who receive letters reply to them. The teacher takes part in the activity as a group member. Writing the letters, delivering them, and replying all take place in focussed silence – very exciting. Here the students secretly and freely choose their addressees, and are themselves chosen.[1]
- The whole class, or those members of it who decide they want to, read what has been written. In a lesson like this students exchange papers or post them up round the walls for others to read. Alternatively, they can write questionnaires for each other.

[1] In classes of fourteen-year-olds, the Markowski technique turns into a sociogram of the sexual stars in the groups. In a group of sixty students that one of us taught, two boys and three girls received a lot more letters than anybody else. On the negative side of this coin are the people who don't get letters. If you happen to be one of these, all you have to do is write someone else a letter. Students receiving letters nearly always feel socially bound to answer them.
A VHS colleague in Baden Württemberg felt so worried about possible marginal people in this exercise that she changed the shape of the activity: in her class each person started off by writing a letter to 'anybody' ('Dear Anybody'). Each letter, though, was signed. These letters were all put on the table in the middle of the room. Each student took one and answered it. This beginning ensures that everybody starts off with a letter to answer.

TOPIC
Students' choice

LANGUAGE
Interrogatives

LEVEL
Elementary to
advanced

TIME
Hard to estimate

MATERIALS
None

6.1 School survey

BACKGROUND
While it is quite possible and satisfying to the students to create a
questionnaire to be administered within their own class, it may be even more
motivating for them to construct one for students in other classes. Sylvie Ogier,
who teaches English in a French lycée, asked her group to brainstorm ideas
for a questionnaire and to select the most popular; they chose to write one
that would give the profile of the typical student in the school. Each student
then wrote three multiple-choice questions as homework, and in a later class
the students voted for the fifteen best questions, which were put together as a
questionnaire for the whole school (320 students). Some of the questions they
chose were:

Do you prefer to spend breaks:
A off the school premises
B in the corridors
C in the schoolyard

To go to your classroom do you prefer:
A to use a lift
B to use the stairs
C to be carried

When you don't like a meal, do you:
A swallow it, pinching your nose
B refuse to eat it
C take it home for your dog

When you think a teacher is bad, do you:
A say nothing and accept her/him
B disturb the lesson
C send a petition to the head

When the questionnaire had been completed and returned, the class made an
analysis of the results. To do this, their maths teacher used the collected data
as the content of a statistics lesson – a very nice example of inter-disciplinary
cooperation.

The advantages of asking students to prepare materials for students in other
classes are many and great. Not the least important is that, in constructing
something for someone else, a feeling of genuine responsibility is created,
which makes the task both more real and better implemented.

In the Ogier model it makes sense for the teacher to check the language
correctness of the finalised questionnaire before it is used.

TOPIC
Survival English

LANGUAGE
Writing practice;
revision of
question forms

LEVEL
Post-beginner to
advanced

TIME
40–55 minutes

MATERIALS
OHP transparency,
wall-chart, or
prepared
blackboard with
five situations
written up. (See
IN CLASS 1 for
details)

6.2 Survival questions

BACKGROUND

'Survival English' is a much-used term. Unfortunately, the survival situations normally considered are within a very narrow frame. In this activity students are invited to look at both the language and the human implications of five rather different situations, not all of which will be within their personal experience.

The steps of the activity follow the familiar 'pyramid' pattern, in which students start by working alone, and then work in larger and larger groups until a conclusion is reached. One advantage for this exercise is that errors can be worked on all through the various stages, with the teacher giving discreet feedback and help.

Asking the group to write twelve questions sounds a lot, but leads them to go beyond the obvious and use their imagination.

IN CLASS

1 Put up the following list of situations.
A a foreign doctor going to work in an African village
B a foreign skier in a Swiss hospital with a broken leg
C a foreign teenager coming to spend a month in an English-speaking country
D a lorry driver crossing foreign territory
E a first-time offender about to start a term in prison (questions directed to an experienced prisoner)
Ask the students, working on their own, to choose one situation and to write twelve questions that would be most useful for the stranger to ask.

2 Ask those who have chosen situation A to pair off and arrive at a joint list of their twelve best questions. Those who have chosen B, C, D and E do likewise.

3 The A pairs form fours and arrive at a common best list. The other groups do likewise.

4 Continue this 'pyramid' process until every student is working in a group that contains all those who chose that situation. This group chooses the six best questions and writes them up on the OHP, blackboard, or on posters round the walls.

5 Allow time for everyone in the class to read all the questions chosen.

<table>
<tr><td>

TOPIC
Memories of early
learning

LANGUAGE
Past tenses;
unhurried
composition

LEVEL
Post-beginner to
intermediate

TIME
25–35 minutes

MATERIALS
Twenty or so small
slips of paper for
each student

</td></tr>
</table>

6.3 Learning to write

BACKGROUND

'Wrong-handed' writing has two functions in this exercise: (a) it makes people immediately aware of the time when writing was physically hard; (b) it slows down their hurry to form questions in the foreign language and so allows them more thinking time to get the grammar right. The silence in which this exercise is conducted also helps with this. Writing with the unaccustomed hand stirs early memories; it feeds the question-asking activity in stage 2 below and fuels the discussion in stage 3. For some people the experience of wrong-handedness is fiercely frustrating and much language flows from the expression of this frustration.

IN CLASS

1 Ask the class to brainstorm the theme of *primary school*, shouting out the words they associate with that phrase to a student secretary who writes them down immediately on the blackboard.

2 Divide the class into groups of five. Give each group eighty or so small, blank, paper slips. Four of the students in each group start writing questions on the slips to the fifth about his/her primary school experiences. The four write their questions 'wrong-handedly' (i.e. left-handers use their right hand and vice versa). This makes them write much more slowly than usual. The fifth group member says nothing, but receives the questions and immediately writes replies (with the usual hand) back to the questioners.

3 Let the silent questioning go on for ten to fifteen minutes. Then bring all the class together and pair them off to tell each other experiences from their primary school days.

Note: You may find this exercise waywardly odd. In this case you won't use it. The trigger we use here is certainly unusual, but *what* it triggers, discussion of early learning, is eminently reasonable for people currently engaged in adolescent or adult learning. Though apparently odd, other-handed writing is a normal and proven therapy technique for allowing people to quickly access areas of their past. What appears odd to us tends to depend on how little we know; for example, in so far as I know almost no Japanese, final question particles in Japanese interrogative sentences strike me as decidedly odd.

Acknowledgement: We first came across a 'wrong-handed' exercise in the work of a USA Pilgrims colleague, Lou Spaventa. He asked his classes to write a dialogue between their right and left hands. Extraordinary dialogues they were too. We then met the idea in G. Moskowitz's *Caring and Sharing in the F.L. Classroom* (Newbury House 1978).

6.4 Silent writing

TOPIC
Project interviews

LANGUAGE
Mixed question forms; confidence-building

LEVEL
Post-beginner to intermediate

TIME
45–50 minutes (first class); 25–35 minutes (second class)

MATERIALS
None

BACKGROUND
Some teachers think that their students' every classroom minute should be filled with productive, and preferably audible, activity. Silence, however, can be both relaxing and productive, especially when the teacher is also silent; the student has time to think, and is released from the obligation to 'perform'.

IN THE FIRST CLASS

1 Explain that you want the group to prepare a questionnaire that they will put to people outside the group. This could be to another class (perhaps at a higher language level), or to foreign tourists whom the students meet in the street, or to foreign personnel on a visit to a factory in your area – wherever the use of English would be appropriate.
If the students are in an English-speaking country, the questionnaire might be put to the people with whom the student is staying, or to those running a local community centre, shopkeepers, etc.

2 Ask the students to work in complete silence; they should come up and write on the blackboard any questions they want to ask the target group. The aim is relevance and grammatical accuracy. If a student sees a language mistake in a question written up by someone else, he/she can come and write a question mark over it, or correct it if he/she is sure what it should be. You as teacher should refrain from correction at this stage, though you may write up one or two questions of your own to introduce useful new idea areas.

3 When there are lots of questions on the board, point to any that are linguistically wrong or obscure. Point silently and get the students to suggest changes.

4 Ask the students to work in pairs and select the fifteen questions they prefer from the mass on the board. Ask the class to suggest polite, prefacing remarks for use in the actual interview, such as 'May we interview you about ...', and suitable 'thank-you' statements. Ask the pairs to add another five questions entirely of their own.

5 Send the students off to do the interviews (individually or in pairs, in class time or as homework, according to the circumstances). Tell them that while they are conducting the interview they should note down the answers given.

IN THE SECOND CLASS

6 The students are asked to work in fours. In each group, one student describes the person she/he interviewed. She/he then assumes the pose of the person interviewed, and hands the interview questions to one of the others, who conducts the interview with the original interviewer answering for the interviewee. The same process is repeated by each student in the group.

Acknowledgement: The idea of silent blackboard work was taught to us in a teacher-training group at Pilgrims in 1978 by Waltraut, an Austrian colleague.

<table>
<tr><td>

TOPIC
Success

LANGUAGE
Vocabulary:
revision; question
forms

LEVEL
Upper
intermediate

TIME
30–40 minutes
(first class);
15–25 minutes
(second class)

MATERIALS
Prepare envelopes
containing the
twenty-four words
and phrases in 1
above, each on a
separate slip of
paper. You will
need one set for
every six students.

</td></tr>
</table>

6.5 Failure and success

BACKGROUND

The first part of this activity uses a vocabulary revision exercise to focus students' feelings about failure and success. The second, through interviewing one another, gives them the opportunity to explore and share their personal successes.

IN CLASS

1 Divide your class into groups of six. Give each group a word envelope containing the following twenty-four words and phrases:

DIVORCE	FAILURE	SUCCESS	FINALS
DEATH	BANKRUPTCY	WORRY	NEVER
ELECTION	HONOUR	TO BROOD	FAME
MEDIOCRE	WINNER	PRESSURE	AWARENESS
PRIZE	GUILT	WEALTH	PUNISHMENT
EXAM	TO GIVE UP	HAPPY	MARRIAGE

Ask them to spread the words on a flat surface. Now ask them, as a group, to organise the twenty-four words into eight sets of three according to meaning. This will usually cause some disagreement.

2 Get the sixes circulating so that they can see how other people have organised their sets.

3 (optional) Invite one student to think of a personal success. Ask him/her to come out in front of the class, together with a panel of two or three questioners. Sit with the panel yourself, and interview the selected student about her/his success. (This type of modelling should be used with care. Don't do it with students who are unaccustomed to coming forward in front of the whole group.)

4 Ask the students to work on their own and bring back to mind a success of theirs. Ask each person to write fifteen to twenty questions that an interviewer might want to put to her/him about this success.

5 Pair the students. Ask them to exchange their question sheets and to interview each other about their successes.

6.6 Advertising questionnaires

TOPIC
Ego-appeal in
advertising

LANGUAGE
Question forms;
imaginative writing

LEVEL
Upper
intermediate to
advanced

TIME
45–60 minutes

MATERIALS
One copy for each
pair of the three
adverts below,
and/or copies of
other
'questionnaire'
adverts you can
find.

BACKGROUND

Advertisers have discovered the egocentric appeal of quizzes and
questionnaires, and are increasingly using pseudo-questionnaires to advertise
their products. Three rather different examples of this technique are offered
here to encourage students to try their hands at producing their own.

Your role as teacher during the students' writing is to act more as a
copy-writing tutor than as an EFL instructor. Don't accept tired language –
demand that they think carefully about the target audience. Make them aware
of the emotional impact of words. Enjoy being other than an EFL teacher.

IN CLASS

1 Pair the students and give each pair a copy of the 'Employers' advert. Ask
  one to play the role of employer and the other to ask the questions.
  (5 minutes)

2 Ask the students to find new partners. Give each pair the 'Ireland' advert
  and ask them to read the statements and decide whether they can possibly
  say no to any of them. (5 minutes)

3 Give the pairs the 'Diners Club' advert and ask one person to administer the
  quiz to the other. Check on the score round the class – the chances are
  that most people will have scored very low. Tell the pairs what their scores
  were, commiserate, and ask what the aim of the questionnaire was. Then
  ask them to imagine (in pairs or small groups) what sort of person might
  score very high on the test. (10 minutes)

4 The students work in pairs or small groups and write pseudo-questionnaire
  adverts.

5 Have the new adverts stuck up on the walls of the classroom so that people
  can read one another's.

Employers.
Test your powers
of hypocrisy.

1. Do you think it's a good idea to give school leavers training and practical experience?
   YES ☐ NO ☐

2. Do you think it's a good idea for *you* to give school leavers training and practical experience?
   YES ☐ NO ☐

3. Would you be only too happy to do so, if only your company was bigger?
   YES ☐ NO ☐

4. Have you ever moaned about the quality of young people who apply for a job?
   YES ☐ NO ☐

5. Wished that the government would do something about it?
   YES ☐ NO ☐

6. And are you willing to help now that the government have set up the new Youth Training Scheme?
   YES ☐ NO ☐

7. Or are you hoping somebody else will make the effort?
   YES ☐ NO ☐

8. Do you have some other excuse, not listed above, for not helping the new Youth Training Scheme?
   YES ☐ NO ☐

9. Would you accept the same excuse from one of your competitors?
   YES ☐ NO ☐

10. Beginning to wish you'd turned over the page?
    YES ☐ NO ☐

© **Longman Group UK Ltd 1988**

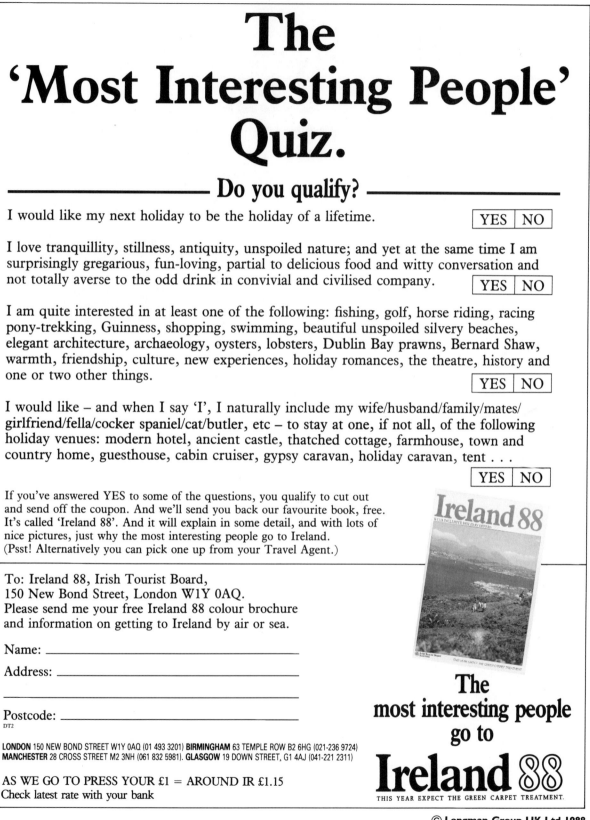

The 'Most Interesting People' Quiz.

Do you qualify?

I would like my next holiday to be the holiday of a lifetime. [YES] [NO]

I love tranquillity, stillness, antiquity, unspoiled nature; and yet at the same time I am surprisingly gregarious, fun-loving, partial to delicious food and witty conversation and not totally averse to the odd drink in convivial and civilised company. [YES] [NO]

I am quite interested in at least one of the following: fishing, golf, horse riding, racing pony-trekking, Guinness, shopping, swimming, beautiful unspoiled silvery beaches, elegant architecture, archaeology, oysters, lobsters, Dublin Bay prawns, Bernard Shaw, warmth, friendship, culture, new experiences, holiday romances, the theatre, history and one or two other things. [YES] [NO]

I would like – and when I say 'I', I naturally include my wife/husband/family/mates/ girlfriend/fella/cocker spaniel/cat/butler, etc – to stay at one, if not all, of the following holiday venues: modern hotel, ancient castle, thatched cottage, farmhouse, town and country home, guesthouse, cabin cruiser, gypsy caravan, holiday caravan, tent . . . [YES] [NO]

If you've answered YES to some of the questions, you qualify to cut out and send off the coupon. And we'll send you back our favourite book, free. It's called 'Ireland 88'. And it will explain in some detail, and with lots of nice pictures, just why the most interesting people go to Ireland. (Psst! Alternatively you can pick one up from your Travel Agent.)

Ireland 88
WITH INCLUSIVE HOLIDAY OFFERS

To: Ireland 88, Irish Tourist Board,
150 New Bond Street, London W1Y 0AQ.
Please send me your free Ireland 88 colour brochure and information on getting to Ireland by air or sea.

Name: _____

Address: _____

_____

Postcode: _____
DT2

LONDON 150 NEW BOND STREET W1Y 0AQ (01 493 3201) BIRMINGHAM 63 TEMPLE ROW B2 6HG (021-236 9724)
MANCHESTER 28 CROSS STREET M2 3NH (061 832 5981). GLASGOW 19 DOWN STREET, G1 4AJ (041-221 2311)

AS WE GO TO PRESS YOUR £1 = AROUND IR £1.15
Check latest rate with your bank

The most interesting people go to
Ireland 88
THIS YEAR EXPECT THE GREEN CARPET TREATMENT.

© Longman Group UK Ltd 1988

If you can answer these questions, then you should answer these.

1. What is the UK dialling prefix from USA?

   ☐ A. 011 44.   ☐ B. 010 04.

   ☐ C. 001 44.   ☐ D. 0101 44.

2. Where are oysters traditional fare at Christmas?

   ☐ A. France.   ☐ B. Portugal.

   ☐ C. Ireland.

3. Which of the following has not been performed at Glyndebourne in the last five years?

   ☐ A. Die Zauberflöte.

   ☐ B. Mayerling.

   ☐ C. The Rake's Progress.

   ☐ D. Der Rosenkavalier.

4. On a business trip to Hungary you find yourself entertaining a client to dinner. He suggests you finish the meal with TUROSCSUSZA. Is it:

   ☐ A. Fruit pancakes.   ☐ B. Baked apple.

   ☐ C. Pasta and curd cheese gratin.   ☐ D. Sour cherry soup.

5. Which of the following cups is competed for at Cheltenham?

   ☐ A. Wightman Cup.   ☐ B. Cowdray Cup.

   ☐ C. Gold Cup.   ☐ D. Ryder Cup.

6. How many working nights abroad qualify you for tax relief?

   ☐ A. 50.   ☐ B. 40.

   ☐ C. 25.   ☐ D. 30.

7. Where was the 1983 British Open held?

   ☐ A. Troon.   ☐ B. St. Andrews.

   ☐ C. Royal Birkdale.   ☐ D. Muirfield.

8. Which of these famous Claret producing Chateaux is not in the Medoc district?

   A. ☐   B. ☐   C. ☐   D. ☐

9. Which Havana tobacco indicates a strong cigar?

   ☐ A. Claro.   ☐ B. Oscuro.

   ☐ C. Maduro.   ☐ D. Colorado.

Answers 1.A 2.A 3.B 4.C 5.C 6.D 7.C 8.B 9.B

If you've answered all or most of the questions above you're doubtless a member of Diners Club International already. If by some oversight you have not as yet joined and are not taking advantage of the Diners Club charge card service, here's your chance to rectify the situation.

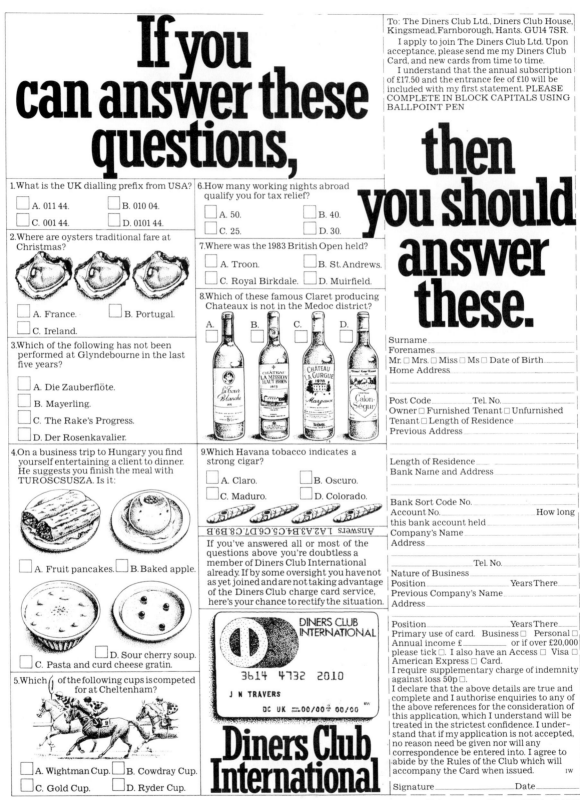

DINERS CLUB INTERNATIONAL

3614 4732 2010

J N TRAVERS

DC UK 00/00 00/00

Diners Club International

© Longman Group UK Ltd 1988

TOPIC
Life difficulties

LANGUAGE
Questions about
the future

LEVEL
Intermediate
to upper
intermediate

TIME
50–60 minutes

MATERIALS
One 'Difficulties'
sheet for each pair
of students

6.7 Thoughts of an unborn child

BACKGROUND
This activity links thoughts of past and future; we have all been children, we
have all had aspirations. The empathetic aspect (see also the note on 'doubling' in
'Oral work', p 81) of the activity makes it very useful in groups where there is
a large age-span.

IN CLASS
1 Pre-teach any vocabulary the students may not know on the 'Difficulties'
  sheet.

2 Pair the students. Give out the sheets and ask them to select the five
  most serious difficulties and rank-order them.

3 Have the students stand up and mill about the room in pairs, comparing
  one another's rank orderings. Allow time for discussion between pairs, but
  insist that the students work with several different pairs.

4 Divide the class randomly into two halves. Students in one group write ten
  to fifteen questions that an unborn baby might want to put to its prospective
  parents. The baby speaks directly to the parents.
  For example: – When I come into the world where will you put me to sleep?
               – Will you breast-feed me?
               – Who will look after me if Mum goes back to work?
               – How long are we going to live in *My* house?
               – Will I have to learn to read?

  Those in the other group write ten to fifteen questions that a prospective
  parent might want to ask an oracle or omniscient being about the child's
  future.

5 Pair the students within each half of the class, and ask each pair to agree on
  the ten best questions out of all they have written.

6 Put pairs from one half of the class (unborn children) with pairs from the
  other (prospective parents). Have them put their questions to each other.

Acknowledgement: The idea for this activity came from a very moving book
by Oriana Fallaci, *Letters to a child never born* in which she talks to the baby
inside her whose birth is in doubt.

'Difficulties' sheet

Which of these life events do you think are most difficult to adjust to? Choose the five most serious and rank-order them.

Outgoings on mortgage or rent of over $20,000 per year

Change of school

Sex difficulties

Change in eating habits

Christmas

Jail term

Son/daughter leaving home

Spouse begins or stops work

Fired at work

Marital separation

Change in sleeping habits

Death of spouse

Vacation

Religious or political conversion

Change in responsibilities at work

Beginning or end of school

Trouble with in-laws

Death of close friend

Pregnancy

Personal injury or illness

Marriage

Retirement

Gain of new family member

Death of close family member

Change in social activities

Change in work hours or conditions

Outstanding personal achievement

Marital reconciliation

Change in health of family member

Change in church activities

Revision of personal habits

Change of residence

Business readjustment

Change in living conditions

Change in recreation

Minor violation of the law

TOPIC Sleeping habits and their psychological significance LANGUAGE Vocabulary: psychological tests; description of sleeping positions LEVEL Intermediate to advanced TIME 45–90 minutes MATERIALS One 'Three interpretations' sheet for each student One 'Eight interpretations' sheet for each student Five extra copies of both that you cut up into separate slips One 'Sleeping cartoons' for each student One 'Objections' sheet for each pair of students

6.8 Sleeping habits

BACKGROUND
(See 1.8)

IN CLASS

1 Give out the 'Sleeping cartoons' sheet and ask each student to identify her/his own most usual sleeping position.
Give out to each student the interpretation, on a separate slip, that corresponds to the cartoon she/he has chosen as fitting her/him.

2 Give out the 'Three interpretations' sheet and ask the student to match these with the corresponding drawings. (The reason for giving out only three interpretations is that these and the one given out in the previous step provide the students with a writing model.)

3 Pair the students and ask them to choose four pictures they do not have interpretations for, and write interpretations.

4 Put the students in groups of six and ask them to read their interpretations to one another.

5 Give them the 'Eight interpretations' sheet and ask them to compare these with their own and with the corresponding drawings.

6 They work in pairs on the 'Objections' sheet, rank-ordering the practical and cultural objections to this psychology test in order of seriousness. If you wish, they could go on to provide spoof interpretations of their own, e.g. 'Your feet stick out below the covers' means 'Your bed is too short'.

Acknowledgement: The test was taken from *Testez-vous vous-même*, by Ghislaine Andreani (Hachette 1978).

Sleeping cartoons

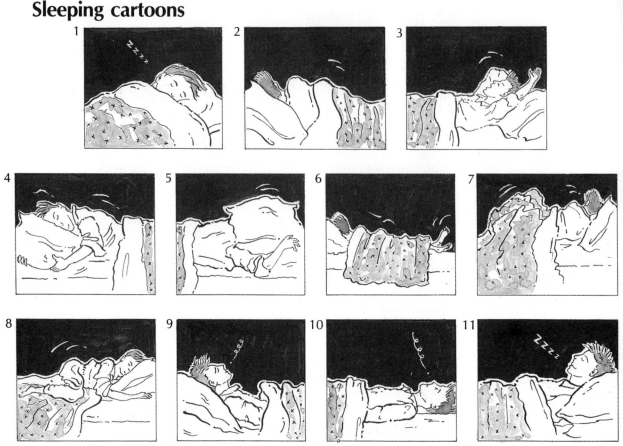

© Longman Group UK Ltd 1988

Three interpretations

If you sleep with your head raised on a couple of pillows

Material well-being is important to you. You are very concerned with comfort and rest. You have a lively intelligence but you are short on physical energy leading to action; you are slightly lazy by nature.

If you sleep with the covers drawn up to your nose

You lack self-confidence but you do nothing to change yourself. By nature you are timorous and always on the alert. On the other hand you like your community and you pay other people a lot of attention. You're very good-natured.

If you sleep with your head under the pillow

You like to be alone, and you are rather strict and hypersensitive. You can never see the middle way. Things are always either black or white. A person is either your friend or your enemy. You tend to pay too much attention to unimportant things.

© Longman Group UK Ltd 1988

Eight interpretations

If you sleep rolled up in the covers

You need to feel protected. You are shy and easily influenced. Sometimes you are not very expansive. You are capable of throwing a tantrum like a child to get what you want.

If you don't sleep with the covers tucked in

You are independent and very active. You put your best foot forward and have no hesitation in your professional as well as in your emotional life. You have a strong personality.

If you sleep on your back, under the covers with everything tucked in

You seem to lack energy and willpower. Maybe you don't want to face life. You often hide your feelings and your thoughts. Your actions are often blocked by your shyness.

If you sleep on your back, without a pillow

You are an idealist – you allow yourself no weakness. You like tight timetables, organised in advance. You would think it below you to try and please others. They have to take you as you are.

If you sleep with your knees bunched up

You regret the passing of your happy childhood. You live nervously, but in continual tension. You often live closed in on yourself but you have a sense of responsibility.

If you sleep with your feet sticking out below the covers

Over the years your lack of order makes you hard to live with. You have a butterfly temperament and you can't cope with constraints. You claim to have no complexes but in fact this is not the case. People round you put up with you most of the time as you are kind and brimming with vitality.

If you hold a pillow in your arms

People think you are strong-willed and independent, but in fact you have been unconsciously fooling them. In love you are fragile; you have a great need for affection and protection. In some ways you lack maturity.

If you sleep on your back with your arms above your head

You are a calm and very active person. You are in full control of yourself. You know yourself well. You don't have doubts about yourself and sometimes you make this felt. You are faithful in love.

'Objections' sheet

Which of the following factors would most interfere with this psychological test making sense?

- The ancient Chinese had porcelain pillows.
- Some people sleep in hammocks.
- In poor families three or four people sometimes have to sleep in one bed.
- In a hot climate people sleep without covers, or with a light sheet over them.
- Some people have backache.
- Some people sleep differently when they have a partner next to them in bed.
- In some cultures babies are swaddled for the first few months of their lives, and so learn to sleep on their backs.
- Some people sleep in great cold, under very heavy covers.
- Traditionally Russians used to sleep on stove-tops in the kitchen.
- Californians sleep on water beds.
- Some people use electric eiderdowns/blankets.

TOPIC
Relationships
within a home

LANGUAGE
Personal pronouns,
adjectives and
possessive forms

LEVEL
Elementary to
intermediate

TIME
25–40 minutes

MATERIALS
None

6.9 Ownership

BACKGROUND
Even people who dismiss astrology as unscientific nonsense have been known to read their horoscopes in the newspaper. This activity works in the same way!

IN CLASS
1 Write up lists of things in your house that belong

   a) to you and no one else,
   b) to you and other people in the house,
   c) only to other people in the house.

Briefly explain your lists.
Mario wrote these things about his house:

   a) *My things*: the garden, beer mugs given to me by Finnish teachers
   b) *Mine and others*: the telephone, my bed, the oak table we eat on
   c) *Things that belong only to others*: the car (my wife's), the Greek vase (my wife's), the high chair (my toddler's)

(Don't use these authorial lists with your students. *You* are the person they relate to – offer them lists of *yours*.)

2 Ask the students, working on their own, to write similar lists.

3 When they look at their own lists, there may be things that puzzle them. Ask them to write half a dozen questions, addressed to *themselves*, about things that puzzle them, e.g.

Mario, why do you effectively keep others out of the garden?
Mario, you used to like cars – why do they feel bad now?
Mario, do you think that Bruno's (the toddler) chair is really his?
Mario, Michael made the oak table – how much does it really belong to him?

Here again, the teacher should do the modelling of the questions – don't use the 'dead' ones above. They are 'dead' because Mario doesn't belong to your group.

4 Pair the students and ask them first to share their lists and then to exchange their questionnaires, so that B puts A's question to A, which A then answers.

Note: There are possibly a number of students who have never consciously thought about problems of ownership and sharing within the home. This unit is aimed precisely at them, since they will be thinking and feeling in an area they have not mentally tramped through in their mother tongue. They will come to this thought area only via the foreign language and have *new* ideas via English. For some this may be a new experience. For those who go on to use English in their studies, the experience will be replicated many times; time and again they will have to grasp an entirely new scientific concept without reference to the mother tongue.

TOPIC
Simple sequencing
tasks

LANGUAGE
Vocabulary:
daily life (written);
mixed questions
(spoken)

LEVEL
Elementary to
intermediate

TIME
20–25 minutes

MATERIALS
One 'Question'
sheet for each
student

6.10 Sequencing

BACKGROUND

This activity gives considerable language support to elementary students
without trying to pre-empt their creativity. Much of the language used will be,
in a very different frame, what they have already encountered, but perhaps
not internalised, in their course books.

No follow-up is proposed for the activity; process is more important than
product here.

IN CLASS

1 Give out the 'Question' sheets and ask the students to work on them
individually. Make it clear that their first and only task at this stage is to
complete the lists, not to answer the questions.

2 Ask the students to stand up and mill about, putting their questions to as
many people as they can. Give them plenty of time to do this, so that they
can discover the various sequences different people have.

Question sheet

Complete the list of items in each question. You may cross out and replace items that are already there, if you wish.

1 In what order do you put on these items of clothing after a swim?

shoes

_____

_____

_____

pullover/sweater

2 The hot water system has broken down. You have to wash the dishes by hand with only one bowl of hot water from the kettle. Which would be the most *stupid* order to do the washing-up in, if you cannot change the water.

pans

brandy glasses

_____

_____

_____

3 In which order do you personally like eating these foods at a meal?

salad

_____

_____

cheese

_____

_____

meat

4 Which sounds do you hear in the morning? Of the ones in the list below that you *do* hear, which order do you hear them in?

birdsong

_____

alarm clock

_____

the noise of kitchen things

_____

_____

the radio

5 If you are trying to start your car, which is the *middle* one of these five actions?

_____

looking in your driving mirror

_____

pressing down the accelerator

_____

6 In what order do babies learn to do these things?

yawning

_____

_____

sitting up

_____

7 When you have woken up in the morning, what are the *first* and *last* things you do from this set?

going to the toilet

brushing your hair

_____

_____

_____

8 When you are going off on holiday, in which order do you usually pack the following things?

_____

socks

paperback

_____

toothbrush

_____

_____

_____

9 When you read a newspaper you know well, which of the following sections do you read and in which order?

_____

editorial comment

_____

book reviews

10 On returning home from a trip, which of the following things will you do and in which order?

read your post

_____

unpack your clothes

_____

_____

_____

TOPIC
Attitudes to the
new and the old

LANGUAGE
Question forms
of all kinds

LEVEL
Elementary to
advanced

TIME
30–45 minutes

MATERIALS
One questionnaire
for each student
A collection of
new objects, old
objects and
'rubbish' (see IN
CLASS 1 for
suggestions)

6.11 Rubbish

BACKGROUND
It can be illuminating to discover that other people's ideas can be *very* different from one's own.

IN CLASS

1 Show the class the collection of objects. Here are some suggestions:
   New objects – a cheap ornament, a toilet roll, a rubbish bag
   Old objects – a small antique, a worn-down pair of shoes, a used piece o carbon paper
   'Rubbish' – an old milk bottle tap, a chicken bone, a used sardine tir (good because of smell)
   Ask them which they reckon are 'rubbish'. General discussion about what 'rubbish' is.

2 Give each pair two copies of the questionnaire. Working together, the pairs enrich the questionnaire, adding one question for every two given. Each partner writes the new questions onto her/his copy.

3 The students then work with a new partner and administer their questionnaires.

4 It may feel right at the end of this class to have a general discussion.

Questionnaire

- How much rubbish does your family produce and put out for the dustman each week?
- Do you sub-divide your family rubbish? If so, into what categories?
- _____

- What happens to old newspapers in your family?
- How long does it take for your toothbrush to become 'rubbish'?
- _____

- How many pairs of shoes do you own? How many pairs are
  a) normally worn
  b) seldom worn
  c) nearly 'rubbish'?
- What happens to food left over at the end of a meal in your family?
- _____

- What do you do with ballpoint pens when the ink runs out?
- Do you often feel guilty about throwing things away?
- _____

- Are there things you positively enjoy throwing away?
- Do you often try to give things away rather than throw them out?
- _____

- Do you ever take things that other people have thrown away?
- Would you like to be a dustman? Why (not)?
- _____

<table>
<tr><td>

TOPIC
Attitudes to cars
and motorbikes

LANGUAGE
Question forms
in any tense

LEVEL
Post-beginner to
intermediate

TIME
40–55 minutes

MATERIALS
None

</td></tr>
</table>

6.12 Cars and motorbikes

BACKGROUND

You will be lucky to get students in a mood for writing questions in a foreign language the moment they come into the classroom. You need to offer them a warm-up. The initial warm-up below is pictorial, a picture produced from within the group.

This is followed by a word brainstorm which begins to build up vocabulary the students may need in writing their questions.

It is only at the third stage of the lesson that the learners start writing questions. We strongly advise you not to offer them model questions at the beginning of this phase. Simply make it clear to them that they are to write the questions they want about cars or bikes. How can you possibly know the questions they will want to write, particularly when they are addressing them to named others in the group?

IN CLASS

1 With an adult group get someone to draw a picture of a car on the board. If you teach adolescents, make it a motorbike or BMX.

2 Have the students brainstorm all the words they know in English connected with cars/motorbikes, with a person at the board to quickly write them down. If the 'secretary' makes spelling mistakes, silently point to the error but leave it to the secretary and the group to correct.

3 Ask each student to write ten to fifteen questions addressed to other class members about the topic. Each question *should carry the name of someone in the group*. Questions addressed to a specific person tend to be much more real than general questions and provoke more committed responses.

4 Tell the students to get up and mill round the room, asking each other their questions. Each question should be put to the person for whom it was written.

VARIATIONS

Instead of using the blackboard you could ask the students to each draw their current car/bike, or one they would love to have.

You could use any topic of interest to the class. Some teachers have found this exercise to be powerful when the topic is *not* one that is normally discussed. We have used parts of the body: feet, hands, etc.

Acknowledgement: We learnt the idea of getting students to prepare questions aimed at specific classmates from Marjorie Baudains. She used the technique for getting secondary students to make up their own comprehension questions round a reading passage. Aiming the questions at definite people made the exercise come to life.

TOPIC
Household
budgeting in
France

LANGUAGE
Noun phrases

LEVEL
Elementary to
advanced

TIME
30–45 minutes

MATERIALS
One 'Household
budget in France
in 1979' sheet for
each student

6.13 Spending patterns

BACKGROUND

One's assumptions about other people's behaviour may be very wide of the mark. Here, a survey of patterns in one country (France) may provide a yardstick.

IN CLASS

1 Write the column of percentages of total expenditure (not in same order) up on the board next to the column of budget headings:

Budget headings	Percentages (not in same order)
Food	9.0
Housing	17.8
Transport	4.8
Clothing	7.8
Household goods	2.7
Culture, leisure, education	8.1
Health	25.3
Holidays	10.2
Miscellaneous	14.3

Ask the students to decide which of the headings go with which of the percentages. They do this in pairs. What they are effectively doing is deciding how they think people in an industrial country spend their money.

2 When they are through, write up the second percentage list, which is the key.

Budget headings	Percentages (in correct order)
Food	25.3
Housing	17.8
Transport	14.3
Clothing	10.2
Household goods	9.0
Culture, leisure, education	7.8
Health	4.8
Holidays	2.7
Miscellaneous	8.1

3 Explain that in the questionnaire used to obtain the above national results, the main budget headings were broken up into sub-headings. For example 'Health' had three sub-headings:

– Consulting the doctor
– The chemist's
– Hospital

Tell them you are going to give them the *number* of sub-headings that came under each main heading. Put these numbers up next to the headings already on the board.

The students' task now is to work in threes and decide on the sort of sub-headings they would expect to see under each main heading.

Budget headings	Sub-headings (exact number)
Food	3
Housing	5
Transport	5
Clothing	5
Household goods	10
Culture, leisure, education	11
Health	3
Holidays	2
Miscellaneous	3

4 Ask the threes to compare categorisations.

5 Give out the 'Household budgets in France in 1979' sheet so they can compare their sub-headings with those dreamed up by the French statisticians.

6 Divide your class into three groups.
   Tell group A they are the breadwinners in a family of four – two parents and two small children. Tell them they have a high income (suggest a monthly or annual sum).
   Tell Group B they are the same as A but they have an average income.
   Tell Group C they are poor (give an unemployment benefit figure).
   Ask the people in all three groups, working in pairs, to decide how they will spend their income.

7 Get pairs from A, B and C to come together and to compare their spending patterns.

Household budgets in France in 1979

Food	25.3%		**Culture, leisure, education**	7.8%
Eating in	22.4		Newspapers, magazines, post	1.2
Eating out (restaurants)	1.9		School expenses	1.1
Canteen	1.0		Radio and TV, etc.	1.0
			Books, records, films	1.0
Housing	17.8%		Sport, open air activities	0.8
Rent and services	4.7		Cafes, games, lotteries	0.8
Gas, electricity, etc.	2.9		Tobacco	0.6
Mortgage repayments	4.2		Going out	0.5
Major repair work	3.9		Toys	0.4
Rates and house insurance	2.1		Child-minding	0.4
Transport	14.3%		**Health**	4.8%
Running costs	6.4		Consulting the doctor	2.4
Car and bike insurance	5.0		The chemist's	2.2
Insurance and road tax	2.0		Hospital	0.2
Public transport	0.6			
Long distance transport	0.3		**Holidays**	2.7%
			Holidays and week-ending	2.1
Clothing	10.2%		Second house	0.6
Clothes	5.6			
Hygiene, beauty	1.5		**Miscellaneous**	8.1%
Shoes	1.4		Income tax	5.4
Jewels, watches, bags	0.9		Personal expenses	1.9
Cleaning and repair	0.8		Life insurance	0.8
Household goods	9.0%			
Furniture	2.5			
Electricals	1.0			
Maintenance materials	0.9			
Telephone	0.9			
Hardware, tools	0.8			
Kitchen and crockery	0.7			
Home help	0.6			
Linen	0.6			
Plants, flowers	0.6			
Animals	0.4			

6.14 Tobacco

TOPIC
Smoking, cancer, profit and tax

LANGUAGE
Register: formal interview

LEVEL
Intermediate to advanced

TIME
25–40 minutes

MATERIALS
One 'Interview' sheet for each pair of students

BACKGROUND

The activity uses a fairly familiar language testing frame (deriving questions from answers) to explore personal and social values.

IN CLASS

1 Explain that a medical journalist has interviewed the chairman of a tobacco company about how he feels about selling carcinogenic drugs. The answer sheet contains the tobacco chairman's answers.

2 Give out the sheets and ask the students to work in pairs and decide what the journalist's questions were.

3 Ask the pairs to compare their completed interviews.

4 Point out that while doctors have been relatively successful in countries like the UK in questioning the rightness of selling carcinogenic drugs such as tobacco, there is much less public and social awareness of the dangers to health of alcoholism. Ask the students to work in pairs, role-playing a medical journalist and the chairman of a wine and spirits company with beer-brewing interests. The interviews should last for five to ten minutes.

Note: There is no 'key' to the exercise, as a variety of questions could be framed to elicit these answers.

'Interview' sheet

1 _____

No, I gave up ten years ago.

2 _____

A major source of enjoyment that helps people stay on an even keel.

3 _____

The answer is quite simple; I am *not* a doctor.

4 _____

No, certainly not – I feel people, members of the public, have a right to choose for themselves.

5 _____

Well of course, I'm not. If I were, I'd put the duty up to where I maximised revenue, but not beyond.

6 _____

Of course we're concerned. We have poured a lot of money into research work.

7 _____

I can't tell you exactly, but a great deal. We have to – our competitors do.

8 _____

Unfair. Do you have similar warnings on cars and cans of beer? Totally discriminatory against us in the industry and against the public we serve.

9 _____

Really that's part of my family life – I'd prefer not to answer. Do you teach yours to ask embarrassing questions?

6.15 The good language learner

TOPIC
Qualities of a good
foreign language
learner

LANGUAGE
Construction of
multiple-choice
questions (this is a
useful skill if you
get your students
to write part of
their own tests for
each other)

LEVEL
Intermediate to
advanced

TIME
45–60 minutes

MATERIALS
None

BACKGROUND
A topic too seldom discussed in the language class is language learning.

IN CLASS

1 Hand out copies or put up on the blackboard or OHP the following:

The good language learner

– is musical
– stretches what he/she knows to cover his/her needs
– is a good listener
– has a retentive memory
– modifies her/his personality in the second language
– is a hard worker
– is relaxed
– is under fourteen years old
– is sympathetic to the people who speak the language he/she is learning

Let the students read through the above statements for a minute or so, then ask them to work together in groups of five or six to improve the list; they might alter or delete statements, or add statements of their own. Allow plenty of time for discussion within each group.

2 Dictate to the class the following example question from a questionnaire designed to discover whether a person is a good language learner or not:

You are abroad.
You are an elementary speaker of the language of the country. You need train information. You have a telephone to hand; the station is two kms away.

Do you: a) walk to the station to look at the timetable?
b) ring up the station with a different question, so as to get some practice before asking what you want?
c) ring the station to ask about train times?
d) rehearse to yourself what you need to say, then pick up the phone and ring the station?

Tell the class that this question is designed to discover whether the learner is good at taking language risks. Ask them how they would score the different answers on a 0–10 scale. Then ask them, working in the same groups as before, to devise questionnaires based on the statements they have already agreed. They should also prepare a scoring system.

3 As a final step, ask each group to make enough copies of their questionnaire so that members of other groups can answer them.

Acknowledgement: The theme of the good language learner is taken from a questionnaire by Paul Meara (*Sunday Times* 6.1.86).

Note: The reason for dictating the above situation and questions to the students is to give them mulling-over time. The time a person spends taking down a dictation is a sort of thought-incubation period.

<table>
<tr><td>

TOPIC
Good and evil in
different
ideological and
religious systems

LANGUAGE
Present simple
and present
perfect tenses

LEVEL
Intermediate to
advanced

TIME
30–45 minutes

MATERIALS
One 'Questions of
conscience' sheet
for each pair of
students

</td></tr>
</table>

6.16 Good and evil

IN CLASS

1 Write these questions up on the board:
   - Have I eaten unclean flesh?
   - Have I assumed that the way I see things is the way my neighbour sees things?
   - Have we stolen from our comrades by evading tax?
   - Have I given to the poor what is their due?

Suggest that the above are questions of conscience for people living in certain ideological/religious climates.

2 Ask your students to each choose to work in a particular ideological/religious frame of reference that they know well, e.g. Catholicism, Socialism, Feminism, Islam, etc.
   Ask students to pair off with someone who has chosen the same or a similar frame. The pairs write ten to twelve questions of conscience starting with Have I ...?/Have we ...?/Do I ...?/Do we ...?
   Have some pairs write on overhead transparencies.

3 Put up some of the transparencies – discuss.

4 Round off the class by giving them five minutes to read a UK Roman Catholic set of questions of conscience. Stress that they are not expected to reveal their answers to anyone.

Note: This exercise is not suitable with all classes. In some multi-national classes it could give rise to cultural/racial friction. On the other hand if you have a class of clear-headed intellectuals it is a jewel of an activity, one you might want to share with the teachers of ethics and of the mother tongue.

Questions of conscience

1 Do I deny myself?

2 Do I eat or drink more than is reasonable?

3 Am I envious, proud or arrogant?

4 Am I lazy?

5 Do I accept suffering and disappointment?

6 Have I used bad language?

7 Have I stolen anything?

8 Have I forgiven other people who have injured me?

9 Have I lost my temper?

10 Have I quarrelled with others, or insulted them?

11 Do I hate people?

12 Have I been guilty of physical violence?

13 Have I been faithful to my spouse?

14 Have I been truthful?

15 Have I damaged another person's reputation by lying about her/him?

16 Am I irresponsible as a parent, letting my children have their own way when they shouldn't?

17 Do I put temptation in my children's way?

18 Do I spend as much money as I should on my family?

19 Do I gamble my money away?

20 Do I look after the elderly in my family adequately?

21 Do I exploit other people, spouse, employer, employees?

22 Do I give help to people poorer than me?

23 Do I nothing about flagrant injustices?

24 Do I drive dangerously?

25 Do I fail to pay bills?

26 Do I drink and drive?

27 Do I cheat others of just payment?

28 Do I use other people for my own ends and advantages?

TOPIC
The students' own
past lives

LANGUAGE
Past tenses

LEVEL
Elementary to
advanced

TIME
30–40 minutes
(first class);
45–60 minutes
(second class)

MATERIALS
None

6.17 Biography writing

IN THE FIRST CLASS

1 Ask the students to work in groups of four and prepare questions to ask you about the following periods in your life (assuming you are now thirty): three to six years old; nine to twelve years old; sixteen to eighteen years old; twenty-seven to thirty years old. Tell them to produce five questions for each period, e.g. (for three to six years old)

What is your first memory?
Did they smack you a lot?
What was your room like?
Who do you remember best from that period?
Nightmares?

2 The students fire their questions at you, period by period. We suggest that this exercise starts in the first class focussed on you for a number of reasons:

a) If the students are willing to talk freely about their own lives, you have to be willing to as well.

b) The depth and interest of your answers provide the students with a model for the homework and the work on themselves in the second class. Leader modelling of this sort will often unknot and unlock a group.

c) You will get a picture of certain of your students from the questions they choose to ask, and this may be of considerable help to you in your further thinking about them and their language problems.

FOR HOMEWORK

Ask the students to write five questions addressed to *themselves* about four periods of three years in their own lives. Ask them to preface each question with their own name like this:

'Mary, how did you feel about your last year at kindergarten?'

In this homework the student is writing questions addressed to herself/ himself. The reason for suggesting they do this is that these questions offer a kind of mapping of the life areas they find interesting in their lives.

IN THE SECOND CLASS

1 Pair the students. Person A puts the questions he/she wrote to herself/ himself to Person B, who answers in terms of her/his own life.

A notes down the answers.

They do the same thing the other way round.

The communication here is complex. As person B listens to A's questions, he/she gets a picture of A's concern about herself/himself, but at the same time has to answer the questions in terms of her/his own life.

2 A now combines her/his notes on B into a biographical sketch and B does likewise for A. This entails asking each other a lot more questions and deciding on the order in which to present the information. It is not inevitable that the ordering will be chronological.

3 Ask the students to put up the biographical sketches round the walls of the room for people to read at their own pace. This last stage means that the sketch writers now have readers and real communication is achieved.

CORRECTION

Put up a blank sheet either side of each biography. The writer of the piece, other students and you, the teacher, are free to correct things that seem wrong on the blank sheets, thus preserving the visual integrity of the piece of writing.

Acknowledgement: The idea of people writing questions with themselves as addressees which they then put to someone else is to be found in *Caring and Sharing in the Foreign Language Classroom*, by Gertrude Moskowitz (Newbury House 1978) and in *Grammar in Action*, by Frank and Rinvolucri (Pergamon 1983).

TOPIC
Rail travel habits

LANGUAGE
Noun phrases

LEVEL
Intermediate

TIME
30–45 minutes

MATERIALS
One copy of the
'Rail users'
questionnaire
for every three
students.

6.18 Rail travel questionnaire

IN CLASS

1 Explain to the students that the aim of this questionnaire is to find out how people use the railways, and what sort of people they are. The questionnaire would be administered on long-distance trains by non-railway staff.

    The students' first task is to complete the sections 1–9 by adding items. Their second task is to construct a final section, 10, that gives a picture of the sort of person the passenger is. Age might be one variable, social class another, job a third, etc. The students work in pairs completing 1–9 and writing 10.

2 The pairs pair, and the completed questionnaires are compared.

3 If you are teaching in the UK you might get your students to use the questionnaire on a train journey as a basis for interviewing people about their travelling habits. Such interviews can be taped and then used in class for listening comprehension work.

    Alternatively you could get your class to use their completed 'Rail users' questionnaire to interview people from another class in the school. The people from the other class would have to be asked to think back to their last train journey and imagine that the questionnaire was being administered on that train.

'Rail users' questionnaire

1 a) At which station did you join this train?

   b) What means of transport did you use to reach this station?
      (Please show *main* method only).

   1. ＿＿＿＿＿＿＿   4. Lift to station (car)

   2. Other train   5. ＿＿＿＿＿＿＿

   3. Underground/metro   6. ＿＿＿＿＿＿＿

2 a) At which station did you leave this train?

   b) What *main* method of transport will you use to reach your final destination once you leave this train?

   1. ＿＿＿＿＿＿＿   4. ＿＿＿＿＿＿＿

   2. ＿＿＿＿＿＿＿   5. On skis

   3. ＿＿＿＿＿＿＿   6. ＿＿＿＿＿＿＿

3 What is the *main* purpose of your journey today?

   1. Company business   4. ＿＿＿＿＿＿＿

   2. ＿＿＿＿＿＿＿   5. ＿＿＿＿＿＿＿

   3. Forces travel   6. ＿＿＿＿＿＿＿

4 Are you travelling:

   1. Alone   4. ＿＿＿＿＿＿＿

   2. With parents   5. ＿＿＿＿＿＿＿

   3. ＿＿＿＿＿＿＿

5 Who bears the cost of your travel ticket for this journey?

   1. Yourself   3. ＿＿＿＿＿＿＿

   2. ＿＿＿＿＿＿＿   4. Your employer

(continued …)

6   a) On which leg of your journey are you now travelling?

      1. Outward ☐   2. Return ☐

    b) How will you be making/how did you travel on the other leg of your journey?

      1. _____   4. _____

      2. _____   5. Hitch-hiking

      3. Sleeping car   6. Plane

7   How did you obtain details of this train?

      1. _____   3. _____

      2. Pocket timetable   4. _____

8   On this journey today, I have used or will use:

      1. Buffet or drinks service at counter   3. _____

      2. _____   4. My own food

9   Please select three of the following reasons which were important to you in making your decision to travel by rail and indicate their order of importance in the right-hand column, e.g. if you consider 'Able to relax' to be the most important reason for using rail, put the number 4 in the 1st Choice Box, etc.

1. _____   4. Able to relax   1st choice   ☐
                                        2nd choice ☐

2. Availability of food   5. Fare paid by   3rd choice ☐
    and drink on the train   someone else

3. _____   6. _____

10

6.19 My ideal teacher

TOPIC
Educational CV

LANGUAGE
Vocabulary:
job applications
and interviews;
revision of tenses,
especially *Did
you ...? How
long have you ...?*

LEVEL
Elementary to
advanced

TIME
60–90 minutes

MATERIALS
One 'Job
application form'
for each pair of
students

IN CLASS

1 Ask the students to imagine that they are going to a summer course in the UK. Instead of the tired administrators of some school over there picking their summer teacher, they can *invent* the profile of the teacher they want.

They work in pairs and fill in the job application form as if they were their ideal teacher. They also add in three to five extra sections, areas not addressed by the original form, and fill these in.

2 *Either*:

Pair the pairs. Ask them to exchange questionnaires and to read each other's in preparation for a job interview. As pair A read through pair B's CV, suggest they jot down questions they want to ask, areas they want to probe, etc.

Pair A go into role as interviewer and pair B go into role as job seeker.

At the end of the interview (fifteen minutes) pair A assess the 'candidate' on a scale of one to ten.

Or:

You, the teacher, have completed the questionnaire either with your own real life details or thinking of the *ideal* teacher you would like to have on a summer course. You do yours on a big sheet or on a transparency.

Show the class your CV. They now probe and interview you.

VARIATION

One of the piloters of this book used this exercise as the inspiration for a full morning's work.

In groups of four to six the students designed an advert for a teaching post and an application form of their own, using the one given here as a stimulus. The groups exchanged adverts and forms. Each student filled in a form (these had been photocopied).

A couple of candidates were selected by each group and these people were given in-depth job interviews. The interviews were recorded so that language work could be done on them afterwards by the teacher.

This is exactly the way we hope *you* will use the book; work out your own lessons from whatever excites you here.

Job application form

1. Higher Education				[Please leave blank]
Qualification	Grade	Date	Where obtained	

2. Experience						
Establishment	Dates	Hours taught per week	Type of Student	Type of Course	Level	Class Size
Teaching General English						
Teaching Business English						
Teacher Training						
Other Work Experience						

3. Other Skills

[Please leave blank]

4. Describe your Present Job

5. As part of our Evening Programme we offer our students a range of $1\frac{1}{2}$ hour seminars on such subjects as 'Ulster', 'Industrial Relations' and 'English Churches'.
Do you feel able to lead such a seminar? ☐ Yes ☐ No
If Yes, on what topics, and what level of English would the students need?

Topic(s)	Level of English

6. Please enlarge on your personal qualities and experience, and say what particular contribution you would hope to make to this school.

7. What Foreign Language(s) do you speak, and at what level?

Language	Level

8. Which Foreign Countries have you lived in, and for how long?

Country	Duration of Stay

9. What are your Leisure Interests and Hobbies?

10. Have you had any Articles or Books published? ☐ Yes ☐ No
If Yes, please list Title(s)

Bibliography

Andreani, G 1978 *Testez-vous vous-même*, Hachette

Augarde, T 1984 *The Oxford Guide to Word Games*, OUP

Baddely, A 1982 *Your Memory*, Penguin

Davis, P *et al.* 1988 *Dictation*, CUP

Ellis, A 1958 Rational Psychotherapy, in *Journal of General Psychotherapy 59*

Ely, P 1984 *Bring the Lab Back to Life*, Prentice Hall

Fallaci, O 1982 *Letters to a Child Never Born*, Hamlyn

Frank, C and Rinvolucri, M 1983 *Grammar in Action*, Pergamon

Hadfield, J 1984 *Communication Games*, Harrap

Howard-Williams, D and Heard, C 1986 *Word Games with English*, Heinemann

Kenny, G and Tsai, B *Sense of Teaching*

KELTIC 1986 *See for Yourself* video (25 Chepstow Corner, Chepstow Place, London W2 4TT)

Ladousse Porter, G 1984 *Speaking Personally*, CUP

Morgan, J and Rinvolucri, M 1984 *Once Upon a Time*, CUP

Morgan, J and Rinvolucri, M 1986 *Vocabulary*, OUP

Mill, C R 1980 *Activities for Trainers – 50 Useful Designs*, University Associates

Moskowitz, G 1978 *Caring and Sharing in the Foreign Language Classroom*, Newbury House

Shepherd, W 1971 *Shepherd's Glossary of Graphic Signs and Symbols*, Dent

Rinvolucri, M 1985 *Grammar Games* CUP

Remocker, J and Storch, E 1970 *Action Speaks Louder; a handbook of nonverbal techniques*, Churchill Livingstone

Saretsky, T 1977 *Active Techniques and Group Psychotherapy*, Jason Aronson, New York

Sion, C (ed.) 1985 *Recipes for Tired Teachers*, Addison Wesley

Simon, S B, Howe, W and Kirschenbaum, H 1972 *Values Clarification*, Hart, New York

Wright, A *et al.* 1979 *Games for Language Learning*, CUP